LUSTING AFTER
PIPINO'S WIFE

A Comedy in Two Acts

by Sam Henry Kass

SAMUEL FRENCH, INC.

45 West 25th Street   NEW YORK 10010
7623 Sunset Boulevard HOLLYWOOD 900
LONDON   TORO

2

For My Father, Peter Kass

IMPORTANT BILLING AND CREDIT REQUIREMENTS

All producers of *LUSTING AFTER PIPINO'S WIFE must* give credit to the Author of the Play in all programs distributed in connection with performances of the Play and in all instances in which the title of the Play appears for purposes of advertising, publicizing or otherwise exploiting the Play and/or a production. The name of the Author *must* also appear on a separate line, on which no other name appears, immediately following the title, and *must* appear in size of type not less than fifty percent the size of the title type.

LUSTING AFTER PIPINO'S WIFE premiered in September, 1991 at the 45th Street Theatre in New York City. It was produced by Primary Stages and directed by Casey Childs.

VINNIE	Joseph Siravo
PATSY	Wayne Maugans
LORRAINE	Alexandre Gersten
RITA	Debra Reissen

CHARACTERS

VINNIE BELL, thirty years of age.

PATSY CONTE, a friend of Vinnie Bell.

LORRAINE SADLER, a woman in her early thirties.

RITA SCARPA, a friend of Lorraine Sadler.

TIME & PLACE

Spring, 1989.

Various locations in a big city.

LUSTING AFTER PIPINO'S WIFE

ACT I

A local bistro. VINNIE is seated at the bar. HE is being served by PATSY, the bartender. In the background on the juke we hear loud Rock 'n Roll music of the 80s. As the music fades . . .

VINNIE. *(To Patsy.)* . . . The essence is to go beyond what you perceive to be there. Because day in, day out, we stay at what we believe to be constant.

PATSY. Sure.

VINNIE. Is it consistent? Maybe . . .

At what level?

The one we feel most comfortable with?

And is that enough? . . . No, of course not.

Your aim is to strike that chord, on a daily basis—

As part of your ritual, your existence . . .

Perhaps you get there, once or twice—

And then what? You fade back.

PATSY. Or perhaps . . .

VINNIE. Or you go on and on, and reach what you determine to be, the pinnacle of that particular period of striving.

Now you believe that you are there—Perhaps this is the truth. Can you maintain it? Do you want to? What choice do you have? You can't just leave it behind— That's

7

abandonment. That's punishable by what? By guilt of the highest degree. So what do you do? And what does she do? And you, and you, and them?

PATSY. My own feeling would be . . .

VINNIE. (*Cutting him off.*) I can't answer that. I can only deal with that which I am faced with. My own what? . . . Lack of self-aggrandizement? My feelings of fulfillment, or there at? Reaching that level of attainment— It's a dangerous thing. By accident, or by carefully laid-out plans— What's the difference? Now you're there. Sink or swim. Too late to consider the alternatives . . . Comfort with failure— Success with the most excruciating pain. Be it by the grace of God— By hard work—

By what then?

I'm telling you, Patsy—it's a very complicated issue.

PATSY. (*Pause.*) What is?

VINNIE. Love.

PATSY. Do you love her?

VINNIE. Who?

PATSY. This woman.

VINNIE. What woman?

PATSY. The woman you were talking about.

VINNIE. It's a concept . . .

PATSY. Oh.

VINNIE. It's a philosophy . . .

PATSY. I see.

VINNIE. I try to execute its beliefs, in a day to day . . .

PATSY. Routine.

VINNIE. Exactly.

PATSY. And with women in such a manner . . .

VINNIE. Highly successful.

PATSY. That's what I want to know.

VINNIE. That's what I'm telling you.

PATSY. And with this . . .

VINNIE. Mind set.

PATSY. And with this . . . Mind set.
And with this, they respond in such a way . . .
In such a positive way?

VINNIE. It heightens the passion.

PATSY. Does it really?

VINNIE. And yet, allows you to keep your distance.

PATSY. Is that possible, Vinnie?

VINNIE. When used properly, you see nothing, but what you want to see. You hear only what you want to hear. You say what you want to say, and say it in such a way that they're convinced it's what they've been longing to hear.

PATSY. Can I play devil's advocate, for a second?

VINNIE. Please.

PATSY. What happens, you meet a woman . . . She comes into this with a similar mind set. She doesn't see, she doesn't hear, and so on. What happens then?

VINNIE. (*Pause.*) I enjoy that sort of situation. A test of wills is a very sexually arousing thing.

PATSY. (*Pouring him another drink.*) Mmn . . .

Scene 2

LORRAINE and RITA are seated on a park bench. EACH holds an ice cream cone.

LORRAINE. I was walking down the street . . .
Our eyes connected. He paused for a moment, and then
offered to sell me fireworks—
Cherry bombs, sizzlers, Roman candles . . .
Said he carried them all.
(*Pause.*) We went for a cup of cocoa, and he told me
about his wife in the hospital. It's terribly sad . . . Off
the record, the doctors have suggested he pull the plug.
RITA. And you believed him?
LORRAINE. No.
RITA. Isn't it terrible to be young and cynical?

Scene 3

LORRAINE is at an art exhibit. SHE stares at a sculpture.
VINNIE walks into view. HE stares at Lorraine, at the
sculpture, and then back at Lorraine.

VINNIE. It's all very exciting, don't you agree?

(*LORRAINE doesn't respond.*)

VINNIE. The vulnerability of it all— Someone
unmasks their feelings, for all to see . . . A display for
strangers to come and gawk. It's such a sideshow
mentality . . . Such an invasion of the senses. (*Pause.*)
Why are you so solemn? I mean, don't get me wrong—I
find it terribly sexy, I love it, but I just don't understand it.

(LORRAINE doesn't respond.)

VINNIE. (*Reading the title of work.*) "The Loneliness of the Descent." What do you think of that title?

LORRAINE. Do I know you?

VINNIE. Does it matter? . . . I mean, what is it that you have to know?

LORRAINE. Please shut up.

VINNIE. I beg your pardon, dear?

LORRAINE. I don't mean to offend you.

VINNIE. Shouldn't you choose your words more carefully? Shouldn't a little more effort, be spent on the thought process? The horse before the wagon, and all that jazz . . .

LORRAINE. Please don't ask so many questions . . . I've thought it over, and I don't want to talk to you.

VINNIE. I'm sorry.

LORRAINE. That's okay.

VINNIE. No, I'm sorry for you . . .

I'm sorry for your character deficiencies, for your lack of warmth, for the general malaise that seems to have ransacked your soul.

I pity you deeply.

LORRAINE. I had an initial dislike for you. I make very quick judgements, and usually they're quite accurate.

VINNIE. I see.

LORRAINE. Your voice came across as being quite shrill. Perhaps it's the acoustics in here.

VINNIE. I don't think I believe you . . .

My name is Vincenzo. My friends call me . . .

LORRAINE. (*Cutting him off.*) I really don't care for
your voice . . .

Outside in the polluted air, the heaviness, the
smut . . .

It may ring differently.

In here—I don't know.

It's slightly piercing.

VINNIE. Excuse me . . . Excuse me . . .

Since we're on first opinions here . . .

Since we're talking initial response—

I find you to be a frigid bitch.

Okay? That's my thinking here.

LORRAINE. That's fine . . .

Now would you excuse yourself?

There's a ringing in my ears—

I truly believe your voice pitch is responsible.

Perhaps I just need some silence.

VINNIE. What are you, an actress or something? Is this
one of those "Method" exercises? They like tell you to go
out into the public domain, and make a fuckin' ass of
yourself? Is that what this is all about? You some kind of
deluded prima donna? Are you an escapee from a mental
institution. Am I on "Candid Camera"? . . . What the
fuck is this?

LORRAINE. I'm asking you nicely now. For God's
sake. Please— Shut your mouth. Just for a minute or so.
I'd really appreciate it. My head feels like it's about to
explode.

VINNIE. Okay, look . . . Let's be friends. Who needs
all this disdain, right? Why don't we go back to your place,
kick back, hash this whole thing out. We'll break it down,
interpret it, see what it all means, what we're really trying

to say to each other. Come on ... Talk to me. Say something honest.

LORRAINE. My first thought is, perhaps your mother didn't breast feed you as an infant. Is that the case here? Could that be part of your problem? Did you not get to suck enough milk?

VINNIE. Wait a second, sweetheart ... Just a minute, here ... Are you talking about my mother?

LORRAINE. That's who I was asking about ... Yes, indeed.

VINNIE. My mother is dead.

LORRAINE. Oh. (*Pause*.) I was just ...

VINNIE. Are you talking about my mother, who's dead?

LORRAINE. Okay, I'm sorry ... This whole situation has gotten out of hand.

VINNIE. Gotten out of hand? You're asking me if I sucked on my dead mother's titties, and then you claim the situation is out of hand?

LORRAINE. Look, let's just ...

VINNIE. Let's just what?

Let's just shake hands?

Let's just kiss and make up?

You bring my mother into this—

My mother who is deceased. Who died on a cot, in the hallway of a filthy hospital ... A pencil in her hand, trying to fill out the medical forms, so a doctor might see her ... So she could receive some attention, some care ... struggling to maintain her dignity, battling to stay alive—for the sake of her children, her grandchildren, never for herself.

Dead at the age of fifty!

For what? So that someone like you can go waltzing
through life, a crooked smile on your face, malice in your
heart, spewing out venom and not caring who it hits—

LORRAINE. I didn't . . .

VINNIE. People have been slain for talking about
someone's mother.

No questions asked. Whacked right out.

But you're above all that, right?

Those rules, they don't apply to you.

You say what you want, feel what you want, do what
you want . . . The hell with anyone who gets in the way.

LORRAINE, (*Gathering her things.*) I don't have to
listen to this.

VINNIE. Nah, you don't have to listen to this.

You've heard it all before.

Robo-Woman, that's you . . .

(LORRAINE exits.)

VINNIE. (*Calls out.*) My dead mother forgives you!

Because the woman was a saint!

(*Pause.*) You hear me, sweetheart? . . . (*VINNIE
regains his composure, and stares pensively at the
sculpture.*)

Scene 4

VINNIE and PATSY doing laundry.
As THEY fold their clothes:

PATSY. And it's a shame, Vinnie . . .

A damn shame.

A man enters into a situation, predetermined by what? By who?

Forced to act accordingly— A certain way. With standards, whatever— I mean, is it necessary? Is it really all so necessary?

VINNIE. You're talking about . . .

PATSY. What am I asking here? To possess the kind of freedom, to what? To stretch, to grow, to realize the potential within . . .

Perhaps without the repercussions coming back to haunt me, in such a way, that this type of human development, natural progression—won't become just a vicious trick to my fuckin' psyche.

VINNIE. (*Holding up a bed sheet for exam.*) How come these stains never come out?

Scene 5

PATSY and RITA on the supermarket checkout line. EACH holds several items.

PATSY. (*Tapping Rita on the shoulder.*) Of course you don't remember me . . .

RITA. (*Turning to face him.*) I don't think so.

PATSY. It was so long ago.

RITA. Was it?

PATSY. Yes.

RITA. When we . . .

PATSY. When we first met . . .

RITA. Yes . . . Of course.

PATSY. Look at me.

RITA. I'm looking.

PATSY. Nothing, huh?

RITA. Like you said, it was long ago.

PATSY. Yes it was.

RITA. (*Pause.*) How long?

PATSY. Eight years.

RITA. That long?

PATSY. All in a day's work?

RITA. At work?

PATSY. Yes.

RITA. We were at work?

PATSY. You were at work . . .

RITA. And where were you?

PATSY. Drowning.

RITA. The beach.

PATSY. You were the lifeguard near parking lot seven . . .

RITA. And you were drowning?

PATSY. At the time, I presumed I was.

RITA. I remember.

PATSY. Yes.

RITA. You weren't very deep.

PATSY. Everything is relative.

RITA. I signaled for you to walk towards the shore.

PATSY. If only life were that simple . . .

RITA. (*Pause.*) But look at you now . . .

PATSY. I'm alive.

RITA. Yes.

PATSY. And you're still saving lives?

PATSY. No, I didn't mean that.
Excuse me, because I think I broke wind.
RITA. Oh.
PATSY. I mean, I'm pretty sure it was me . . .
Wasn't it?
RITA. Oh . . .
Yes. I mean, I guess it was.
PATSY. I'm a little nervous.
RITA. Don't be nervous.
PATSY. Why not?
RITA. There's nothing to be nervous about.
PATSY. Everything's okay?
RITA. Sure.
PATSY. That's good. (*Pause*.) So you're not a lifeguard
more?
RITA. I'm a social worker.
PATSY. A social worker, huh?
RITA. Yes.
PATSY. That must be real interesting . . .
RITA. It's interesting.
PATSY. Yeah, I bet . . . Working with people . . .
ing to help . . . People. It's a real people job, no?
RITA. I'm around a lot of different people.
PATSY. Yeah.
RITA. (*Pause*.) What kind of work do you do?
PATSY. Pardon?
RITA. Where do you work? . . .
mean, you don't have to tell me, if you don't want to.
PATSY. No, no . . . That's okay.
m a bartender. Part-time.
RITA. Oh . . .
at's a people job, too.

RITA. No . . . It was just a summer job. I was
younger then.
PATSY. Me too.
RITA. (*Pause*.) It's great to see you . . .
PATSY. After all these years, huh?
RITA. Really.
PATSY. Still have that orange bathing suit?
RITA. No . . . I had to turn it in.
PATSY. The white helmet, too?
RITA. Yes.
PATSY. That's too bad.
RITA. Yes.
PATSY. (*Pause*.) I don't know what else to say.
RITA. Oh . . .
PATSY. The line is moving.

(*THEY move up slowly.*)

Scene 6

VINNIE at the bistro. HE is addressing an employee.

VINNIE. Hey, Pipino! My main man!
Right on time . . . Every day, right on time.
God bless you, huh?
Are you the best dishwasher in town, or what? I think
so . . .
Go ahead, I won't bother you. I know how it is, when a
man's trying to work—he don't need those interruptions.

Gotta concentrate, right? That's right, Pipino. You're alright in my book.

(*Pause.*) How's the wife and kids? Everything okay at home? what do you have? . . . Ten, twelve kids, right? God bless you.

You're a good man.

You get laid every night, or wha'?

The wife don't complain, or nothin'?

You got some fuckin' life, huh, Pipino?

What happens? . . . You come home, and give it to her when she's asleep?

Why not, right?

(*Pause.*) You don't understand a fuckin' word I'm saying, do you?

Don't smile at me like an idiot.

Since you don't understand me, I'm going to say one more thing . . .

I'm the manager, you're the dishwasher.

You go home, get laid every night—

I go home and pull off, thinking about how you're getting laid.

Never mind . . .

Pipino, my man— Don't come in here with a translator, asking for a raise. You hear me? 'Cause you're already living the American Dream.

Scene 7

PATSY and RITA in bed, post-coitus; at Patsy's apartment.

PATSY. By the way, I'm Patsy . . .

RITA. Yes, I know.

PATSY. Yeah, well . . . I wasn't sure don't . . .

RITA. My name is Rita.

PATSY. Rita.

RITA. Yes.

PATSY. Oh . . . (*Pause.*) That's a nice

RITA. Thank you.

PATSY. What about my name?

RITA. What about it?

PATSY. It's sort of silly, huh?

RITA. No . . . I don't think so.

PATSY. You like it?

RITA. It's okay . . .

PATSY. Yeah, it's okay . . . (*Pause*

gave it to me.

RITA. Oh.

PATSY. I mean, it's not a nickname that.

RITA. Yes, I understand.

PATSY. (*Pause.*) You got enough blan

RITA. Yes, I'm fine.

PATSY. 'Cause you can pull it over m

RITA. I'm fine.

PATSY. I know how it is with bl people need a lot, some just a little, som either way . . .

Excuse me.

RITA. Oh, that's okay . . .

I swear all the time.

PATSY. Sure it is.

RITA. Do you like it?

PATSY. I like it, but I need something a little more secure.

A little more stable.

That's just the kind of guy I am.

RITA. What kind of work are you looking for?

PATSY. Pardon?

RITA. I mean, you don't have to tell me.

PATSY. No, no . . . That's okay.

It's just a reflex.

RITA. Oh.

PATSY. I'm going to be a shoe salesman.

I'm going to sell shoes.

RITA. That's nice.

And it's also a people job.

PATSY. Sure it is . . .

Everyone needs shoes.

RITA. What store are you going to be at?

PATSY. Pardon? . . .

RITA. I'm sorry . . .

PATSY. No, no . . . I'm going to be working out of my car. Door to door, flea markets, stuff like that. This way I get to be my own man.

RITA. Is that important?

PATSY. Be mg my own man?

RITA. Yes.

PATSY. (*Pause.*) No, not really.

RITA. (*Pause.*) Well, I better be getting dressed. Have to be at the office by nine.

PATSY. Okay.

RITA. Could you just close your eyes, while I run into the bathroom? My clothes are over there, near the bathroom.   And I . . .

PATSY. (*Turning his head.*) Oh, I understand. No problem.

RITA. I mean, can you really close your eyes?

PATSY. You mean, really close my eyes . . . ?

RITA. Yes.

PATSY. Not just turn my head.

RITA. I would appreciate it.

PATSY. No problem.

(HE does as bid. RITA quickly darts from the bed, grabs her clothes, and disappears into the bathroom.)

PATSY. (*Calling out.*) I didn't see anything.

RITA. (*From bathroom.*) I hope you don't find me foolish.

PATSY. No, no . . . That was a very classy move. Many girls, I believe, would not choose to do that. (*Pause.*) I think if I told my mother that, she would find it admirable.

RITA. (*Sticking her head out the bathroom door.*) Please don't tell your mother.

PATSY. My mother and I are quite close.

RITA. Promise me, you won't tell your mother.

PATSY. I promise.

RITA. (*Closing the door.*) Thank you . . . (*SHE reopens the door.*) You're a man of your word, aren't you?

PATSY. (*Pause.*) I believe I am.

RITA. That's refreshing.

Scene 8

LORRAINE and RITA sitting on a park bench. THEY are sharing a bag of popcorn.

RITA. We met many years ago—I saved his life, or so he claims.

LORRAINE. What do you do for an encore?

RITA. I don't know . . . I've never gone beyond saving a man's life. Is there more?

LORRAINE. They think there is.

RITA. Do I detect a note of hostility?

LORRAINE. Against whom?

RITA. Patsy.

LORRAINE. Patsy?

RITA. Yes.

LORRAINE. Is that his name?

RITA. What's wrong with it?

LORRAINE. Nothing . . . Let's change the subject.

RITA. Alright.

LORRAINE. (*Pause.*) I'm thinking about getting a gun.

Scene 9

A street corner. VINNIE walks while reading a newspaper. PATSY and RITA turn the corner, and stumble into Vinnie.

PATSY. (*Taken aback*.) Vinnie . . .

VINNIE. Is this the smallest of worlds, or what?

PATSY. (*To Vinnie*.) This is Rita.

VINNIE. This is Rita?

PATSY. Yeah.

VINNIE. I can't believe it. (*HE takes her hand and kisses it*.) I can't believe it . . . Truly, I can't believe it.

PATSY. (*To Rita*.) This is Vinnie . . .

Remember, I was telling you about him?

RITA. Yes . . . Hello, Vinnie.

VINNIE. He was telling you about me?

Come on, what did he say?

RITA. That you were a friend of Patsy's?

VINNIE. (*To Patsy*.) Is she a diplomat, or what?

PATSY. Yeah, she's great.

VINNIE. Of course she's great . . .

Why wouldn't she be great?

Don't ever sell yourself short, Pats. Remember what I'm saying here—you're great, she's great . . .

Greatness finds company.

No difference than misery.

You both understand what I'm saying here?

PATSY. Sure.

VINNIE. So where you two headed?

RITA. We're going for brunch . . .

VINNIE. Brunch, huh? . . .

That's always confused me.

What exactly is that?

I mean, is that the meal, or the conversation, or the actual hour of the day?

Come on, Rita . . . I'm a caveman. Help shed some light.

RITA. I suppose it's the meal . . .

A combination of breakfast and lunch?

VINNIE. God bless you . . . You're not sure either.

Alright, doesn't matter. It's a phase, a trend, a momentary lark . . . I like to keep it simple. I'm going to eat, I'm not going to eat. No questions there, right? Simple, concise, to the point.

PATSY. Would you like to join us?

VINNIE. I couldn't.

PATSY. (*Looking at Rita.*) Really . . . We wouldn't mind.

VINNIE. You wouldn't mind?

Who am I, old Aunt Yetta?

I'll wait till you can't live without me.

PATSY. No, no . . . We really . . .

VINNIE. Hey, I'm kidding.

Patsy, I'm joking.

(*To Rita.*) The kid has no sense of humor.

You should work on that a little.

The truth is, I'm busy now. I got an agenda. I'll take a raincheck.

PATSY. Okay.

VINNIE. Where you goin' to be, just in case . . .

RITA. The Parisian?

VINNIE. French food? Pats, you going continental on me?

RITA. It's just a coffee shop.

VINNIE. I'm just fuckin' around.

(*To Rita.*) Believe me, I've been all over the world.

RITA. I'd like to travel one day.

VINNIE. Then you will. That's how these things work out.

RITA. I suppose.

VINNIE. Hey, I gotta run now.

PATSY. You sure you don't want to join us?

VINNIE. Come on . . . These are your wonder years. Talk to each other, learn about each other, don't be afraid to be alone. Very important. Know yourselves, know each other. Okay?

RITA. Okay.

VINNIE. (*Pause.*) So what do you do, Rita?

And then I gotta run.

RITA. I'm in social work.

VINNIE. Aren't we all . . .

(*Pause.*) No, I'm kidding. That's very good. Very nice.

What do you do, help place poor people in those hotels?

RITA. That's only part of it.

VINNIE. 'Course it is . . .

Nothing can be summed up in a nutshell.

More than black and white . . . A lot of gray area here.

Plenty of gray.

PATSY. (*To Rita.*) I told you he was a real interesting guy . . . Didn't I?

RITA. Yes, you did.

VINNIE. Did he tell you that, Rita?

He honestly told you that, huh?

RITA. Yes . . .

VINNIE. Isn't he a sweetheart?

What a nice thing to say.

(*Pause.*) You don't usually hear guys talk that way 'bout one another. Especially, there's a lovely young lady involved.

RITA. What do you mean?

PATSY. He just . . .

VINNIE. (*Cutting him off.*) You see, men are cut from a different loin of cloth . . .

They don't usually create a scenario that many times throughout history, has come back to haunt them.

A man is with a woman, as Patsy seems to be with you . . . He meets his best friend on the street, introduces him to the mystery woman. The woman already has a semblance of knowledge, concerning the aforementioned best friend: that he's "a real interesting guy." So already the groundwork is laid . . .

Perhaps there's some sort of initial chemistry between the friend and the mystery woman. Perhaps it's so buried, so hidden, that neither one even recognizes its presence. Perhaps these two newly introduced creatures of our societal jungle—will bid each other farewell, after only minutes of introductory chit-chat, only to go through the remainder of that day, and the following day, and then who knows how many days after, only to be burdened with the sexual magnetism that makes two people prisoners of passion . . .

(*Pause.*) More than likely, that fire eventually burns out. And all that remains are ashes, of what might have been . . .

However, there are those occasions, as history has documented—where these two benighted and tortured souls have no choice but to seek each other out—find one another, track each other to the earth's end, because there is no other choice.

The human being is a very complicated situation. Should never be glossed over, with a wave of the hand. The powers they must wrestle with are stronger than each of us individually . . .

(*Pause.*) Just some food for thought. And, Patsy? . . .

PATSY. Yeah, Vin?

VINNIE. You are a special type of guy.

PATSY. Thank you.

VINNIE. You're welcome.

Scene 10

PATSY knocks on the door of Rita's apartment. LORRAINE is on the other side of the door.

LORRAINE. (*Hearing the knock.*) Yes? . . . Who is it?

PATSY. Hi . . . It's Patsy.

LORRAINE. (*Checking the peephole.*) Who is it, please?

PATSY. Rita, it's me . . . It's Patsy.

LORRAINE. (*Through the door.*) Rita is not here now.

PATSY. (*Trying to see through peephole.*) Oh . . . She does live here, doesn't she?

LORRAINE. She lives here, but she's not here now. Please go away . . .

PATSY. She wasn't expecting me, but I thought I'd surprise her.

LORRAINE. (*Walking away from the door.*) She doesn't like surprises.

PATSY. How do you know? ... (*HE gets no response. KNOCKS on door again.*) Excuse me ... Excuse me ...

LORRAINE. (*Through the door.*) Look, Pasta ... I'll tell her you were here. Could you move away from the door, please?

PATSY. The name is Patsy!

LORRAINE. Fine ... I'll make a note of that.

PATSY. Do you live here?

LORRAINE. I'm inside, aren't I?

PATSY. What's your name?

LORRAINE. Please move away from the door. This is the last warning.

PATSY. What seems to be the problem here? I'm not a criminal. Hasn't Rita mentioned my name to you?

LORRAINE. (*Removing a gun from her purse.*) One ...

PATSY. Could I ...

LORRAINE. (*Pointing it at the door.*) Two ...

PATSY. Could I just ...

LORRAINE. Three. (*SHE pulls the trigger. Nothing happens.*)

PATSY. Could I just come in for a second? I'd like to leave a note.

(*SHE pulls the trigger again—still nothing ... SHE shakes the gun several times. On the other side of the door, PATSY just shrugs his shoulders, and quietly walks away. LORRAINE points the gun at the door, and once more pulls the trigger. This time the GUN FIRES, exploding into the door. SHE listens for a moment at the door, and hears nothing. Very calmly, LORRAINE puts the gun back in her purse, sits down on the couch, and thumbs through a magazine.)*

Scene 11

VINNIE and PATSY at a parking lot flea market. THEY are BOTH sitting on folding beach chairs. A small table, holding samples of Patsy's shoes, stands before them.

PATSY. (*Talking to an imaginary customer.*) Which one? The brown one at the end?

That's an Italian leather. From Palermo.

That's an imported shoe. Very good shoe.

No, not especially comfortable . . .

I have to be honest. A good shoe, a really good shoe— it should not be comfortable. When your foot really hurts, then you know you got a good shoe.

Yeah . . . Twenty-three dollars. Yeah . . .

Okay. Thanks for stopping by.

Have a good day.

(THEY watch the customer walk away.)

VINNIE. Now you're getting the hang of it.

Scene 12

LORRAINE is stretched out on her therapist's couch. SHE speaks to an imaginary therapist.

LORRAINE. I'm just so . . .

I'm just so . . . So what? Could you help me, here? I'm just so what?

Obviously I'm having a little difficulty filling in the blanks—completing the thought process.

So you're the doctor. What the fuck am I trying to say?

I mean, you are a doctor, aren't you? Do you have a degree? Do you have an answer?

Okay, look . . . I believe all the answers are out there for me. The problem is . . . The problem has been, that I've failed to recognize them. I'm sure they've all but slapped me in the mouth— And I just don't see it. Do you know what I'm saying? It's one thing not to have any idea what I'm looking for—it's another to realize I'm looking for something, to possibly know what it is, to feel it's there . . . Right there . . . And yet . . . And yet, what?

(*SHE sits up.*) What are you, a fuckin' mute?

What's the point of all this— To see how many stupid things you can get me to say? You know I'm not making any sense, I know I'm not making any sense, we'll both seemingly never find out, if you have any sense at all . . .

One more thing—I've been meaning to say this for several weeks now . . . There's a severe odor emanating from your side of the room. It's probably affecting my thought process— Some individuals are highly sensitized to smell. This sort of problem has not received enough publicity in the medical journals . . . A doctor who stinks— Someone who has a death-like stench about him can bring on some form of mental incapacity in a patient . . . Sometimes without the patient's knowledge. This is absolutely true.

On one hand, please don't take it personally. And on the other hand, you must do something to rectify the problem. No, no . . . Cracking the window will not solve the problem here. I'm talking about my fuckin' sanity. Do you understand! You must take a shower! You must clean yourself carefully! You are dealing with a human being here. I am not cattle . . .

(*Pause.*) Yes . . . Okay . . .

(*SHE stands up.*) See you next week.

Scene 13

Patsy's apartment. RITA and PATSY are in bed.

RITA. I just feel we've reached that next level . . . That higher plane. You've made me so happy, Patsy— A woman can't express such a feeling, such a . . .

PATSY. It was nothing . . .

RITA. Your love was so honest, so real . . . There were no barriers. And I feel as if you have bared your soul to me.

PATSY. You're absolutely correct.

RITA. My head is spinning ... (*Pause.*) Have I told you how much I love you?

PATSY. No, never ... I don't believe so.

RITA. And I bet you're the best shoe salesman in the entire world.

PATSY. I think I have some potential.

RITA. And I am your woman.

PATSY. Oh ... That makes me happy.

RITA. And I'm so proud.

PATSY. Yes you are.

RITA. And you have confided in me ... In a very spiritual way, you have shared your trust.

PATSY. It was the thing to do, considering the circumstances.

RITA. And what were those circumstances?

PATSY. You don't know?

RITA. I want to hear it from you.

PATSY. Why, the ties that bind, of course.

RITA. How silly of me ... Of course.

PATSY. (*Pause.*) So you're happy, huh?

RITA. And I shouldn't be?

PATSY. You've got it all.

RITA. And more ... (*SHE kisses him.*) I always wanted a shoe salesman.

PATSY. Is this true?

RITA. Deep down, I believe it is.

PATSY. This is stupendous ... Who can I tell?

RITA. My mother will be so happy.

PATSY. She deserves happiness.

RITA. Do you mean that?
Do you really mean that, Patsy?

PATSY. (*Pause.*) I'm not sure.

RITA. Oh.

PATSY. I mean, we've never even met. Everyone deserves happiness— It's just . . . It's just that I don't know her. If I knew her then . . . I just have to be honest.

RITA. A man has to be . . .

PATSY. . . . what he has to be.

RITA. Surprise me . . . What comes next? What can we do for an encore?

PATSY. What do you give the woman who has everything?

RITA. A baby.

PATSY. (*Pause.*) I beg your pardon?

RITA. It would make this situation complete . . .

PATSY. Quite frankly, this situation is very complete. I have my shoes, you have me—

Greed is a very dangerous thing. (*PATSY gets up, starts to dress.*)

RITA. Where are you going?

PATSY. Why to work, of course . . .

RITA. But it's the middle of the night.

PATSY. One must strike when the iron is hottest.

RITA. Who will come and buy shoes, at an hour like this?

PATSY. How can I answer that?

RITA. Do you really have to go?

PATSY. In a manner of speaking.

RITA. What about a baby, Patsy? It's something I want so badly.

PATSY. But we hardly know each other.

RITA. What's to know? . . .

PATSY. But why a child, when you already have me?

RITA. A woman needs a child ...

PATSY. And a man needs a woman.

RITA. Then we will both have our needs ...

PATSY. And that will satisfy you?

RITA. Yes ... I believe it will, Patsy.

PATSY. (*Pause.*) Such a dangerous assumption, Rita.

RITA. What is dangerous?

PATSY. (*Ready to leave.*) To feel that one finishing touch, is the icing on the cake ... It finalizes our dreams, our aspirations. Something that means so much, should probably never be attained. Because that ends the dreaming, Rita. And when the dreaming ends, what's left to hope for?

RITA. Is this true?

PATSY. I'm quite sure it is.

RITA. (*Pause.*) So it shouldn't be that important to me? ... A baby shouldn't be that important?

PATSY. That's up to you ... After all, you're a very modern creature.

RITA. And when it's not an obsession anymore— That will be the time to have my child?

PATSY. It's a tricky proposition ... If it's no longer an obsession, is it still worth dreaming about? And if it is, is it still possible to dream? It's a tangled web one weaves here, isn't it? (*Pause.*) I have shoes to sell, Rita, darling ...

RITA. I'm slightly confused, Patsy ...

Is that okay?

PATSY. It's much more than okay ... (*Pause.*) Don't forget to lock up, when you leave.

(HE exits. RITA sits up in bed, a puzzled and painful expression on her face.)

Scene 14

VINNIE and PATSY sitting on the park bench, eating lunch.

VINNIE. So what's what, with this girl?

PATSY. Rita?

VINNIE. So what's what with her?

PATSY. She's alright.

VINNIE. She's alright, you're alright, everyone's alright, huh?

PATSY. She wants to have a baby.

VINNIE. Alright.

PATSY. That doesn't bother you?

VINNIE. Does she want to have it with me?

PATSY. No.

VINNIE. Then why should it bother me? *(Pause.)* Did she actually say she didn't want to have it with me?

PATSY. No . . . why would she say that? She was talking about me.

VINNIE. 'Course.

PATSY. I think it's just like one of those womanly urges. It'll probably pass.

VINNIE. Everything passes . . . Give it enough time, everything passes. That's what's wonderful about life— Anything you don't want to hear, don't want to see, eventually it passes.

You run any background check on this girl?

PATSY. Background check?

VINNIE. What do you know about her? . . . Family, money, mental illness . . .

PATSY. She's a good girl.

VINNIE. Sure she is . . . I mean, I seen her on the street with you, I say to myself, "She's a good girl." Because she appears to be that way. And because I want her to be as such . . . Because you're my friend. However, that doesn't necessarily make it so. So what exactly do you know about her?

PATSY. Just general stuff . . . She seems to be okay.

VINNIE. I touched a nerve here, huh?

PATSY. No, not at all.

VINNIE. I'm going to butt out.

PATSY. You don't have to butt out— There's nothing to apologize for.

VINNIE. I'm not going to apologize—I'm just gonna mind my own business here, leave semi-well enough alone, keep a separation of church, state, and friendship . . . You want that pickle?

PATSY. You can have it.

VINNIE. (*Takes the pickle.*) Okay, just one more thought here . . .

Just one more thought, and then I say nothing more— Only because you're my friend . . .

You meet this girl. That's wonderful. God bless you both . . . However, prior to you, the girl has had a life. Maybe not much of a life, maybe something different, I don't know. But you don't know either. The girl has been places, said things, seen things, done things . . .

Now she comes to you, and thinks the slate is
automatically wiped clean.

Not so . . .

Maybe on the surface, but not in reality.

Don't get fooled into believing you and her equal square
one . . .

History keeps records on such matters. The reason she's
with you? Fate? Destiny? Something else? . . . I don't
know, you don't care. Does she know? Maybe yes,
probably no, but margin for error on either side.

I'm finished now, alright?

Keep one eye here, one eye somewhere over there.
Understand what I'm saying?

PATSY. Sure.

VINNIE. This all might be meaningless . . . In that
case, no great loss. What's wasted? Some words between
friends. On the other hand, possibly this has been fruitful.
Either way, no charge. (*VINNIE stuffs the last piece of
sandwich into his mouth.*)

Scene 15

*LORRAINE and RITA at their apartment. LORRAINE is
dressed in army fatigues and orange colored hunting cap.*

LORRAINE. Why don't you just come right out and
say it . . . ?

What's with all the secrecy?

Let's just talk, okay?

I mean, whatever happened to talk? Everything is a game now. Everything has some sort of covert, mind-altering, manipulative angle . . . All I want is some truth. That's all I want out of life.

Come on, let's just talk. Nothing else.

RITA. What do you want to know?

LORRAINE. Okay, there we go . . . That's a start. "What do I want to know?"

I don't know . . . Anything. Anything at all.

Let's start trivial. I don't know . . .

Do you suck Patsy's dick? I don't know, let's just talk. Throw out a subject, and we'll just rap a little.

RITA. Do I suck his dick? What kind of question is that?

LORRAINE. Questions are not my strength, okay? Don't hold it against me. Let's just get some dialogue going. Nice and easy, just like the old days.

RITA. Are you okay, Lorraine?

LORRAINE. No, I'm not okay . . . But don't worry about it. Let's just talk through it— Work it out . . . Keep the air littered with sounds. It's very therapeutic. Really, I know what I'm saying here.

RITA. Why are you wearing that hat?

LORRAINE. I'm a little chilly, that's all. Don't look beyond what's there . . . Really. My head is a little chilly.

RITA. Okay.

LORRAINE. What else?

RITA. I don't know . . .

LORRAINE. Anything at all.

RITA. I haven't sucked his dick.

LORRAINE. Why not?

RITA. I don't know ... It hasn't really been necessary yet.

LORRAINE. Okay, what else? ...

RITA. I don't know ... How's work?

LORRAINE. I'm a para-legal ... How's work gonna be?

RITA. I don't really know ... I'm just ...

LORRAINE. (*Cutting her off.*) Work sucks ... I mean, what kind of question is that? They make me wear mohair suits, with high-collared shirts ... Okay?

RITA. I'm sorry.

LORRAINE. What are you sorry about? Your job is worse. What do you do, hand out food stamps?

RITA. You don't have to put down my job.

LORRAINE. Someone should crack those rose-tinted glasses of yours ... Why don't you wake up and smell the dog shit. There's no wonderful existence out there. You're not enjoying yourself, chasing rainbows, creating perfect karma, making this world a better what? ...

None of those things are happening here. Who are you fooling? Do you honestly think that you're any happier than me? Any more satisfied? Because you're not ... You're just as miserable as me, just as miserable as the next guy, just as miserable as Patsy, whose dick you are not sucking ... So please— Just wipe that stupid age of Aquarius smile off your face. Alright? You are not a content or happy individual. Please remember that. Life doesn't dictate that, and you're no exception.

The cat's out of the bag here, and the jig is up. Act as miserable as you really are. Believe me, you'll be a happier and better person for it.

Scene 16

VINNIE and PATSY, lounging in a health club sauna. THEY are BOTH clad only in towels.

VINNIE. (*Slapping his stomach.*) Stinks in here a little, no?

PATSY. Not too bad.

VINNIE. It's okay?

PATSY. Yeah.

VINNIE. This don't bother you?

PATSY. (*Slapping his stomach.*) Ah . . .

VINNIE. Wouldn't hurt a little— They came in here every morning, maybe toss a little Lysol around. Maybe they could do that, and it wouldn't kill them.

PATSY. You have to relax a little.

VINNIE. I would like to relax.

PATSY. Very important—from a health standpoint, it's a very important thing.

VINNIE. To relax.

PATSY. Very important, Vinnie.

VINNIE. I would like to relax . . .
It's one of the things I would like to do.
Only so many hours in the day.

PATSY. Do some deep breathing.

VINNIE. I should do some deep breathing?

PATSY. Come on . . . In and out.

VINNIE. In and out, what? Smells like one giant asshole in here. You want me to pass out, crack my head on the fuckin' tiles? Paramedics come in here, carry me out

with a towel dangling from my waist? Lemme just catch
my breath here . . .

*(HE exits, leaving PATSY in the sauna area. Seconds later,
VINNIE returns.)*

VINNIE. *(Looks shocked.)* When did the locker room
turn co-ed? We came in here twenty minutes ago, it was a
men's locker room . . . Right?
PATSY. Yeah . . . What are you talking about?
VINNIE. Take a look through the window . . .

(PATSY gets up to look.)

VINNIE. Go 'head, take a look. Maybe the air is
making me dizzy, or somethin'. That ain't a woman
getting dressed in there?
PATSY. *(Looking through glass.)* This is very
strange . . . She's like a woman— But she's like a man
too. Take another look.
VINNIE. I don't want to take another look. *(Pause.)*
What are you sayin'? Like half-man, half-woman? Like
half and half? . . . I'm getting fuckin' dizzy in here, I
swear to God.
PATSY. Just take a quick look.
VINNIE. *(Looks through glass.)* What's this world
coming to? She's like between operations, or somethin'.
Like he/she went in for a knife job, found out midway
through she had no money, and they just stopped the
job . . . Right there in the middle, they just stopped.
    What kind of club is this? Nobody told me I had to read
the fine print. They ask you to sign, so I signed. Nobody

told me I had to read through the whole agreement. (*Pause.*) This is like a head trip I'm not really prepared for. And between the steam and the stink, I'm about ready to faint.

PATSY. Just try to relax, Vinnie.

VINNIE. Fuck you with that relax shit, already . . . I come in here trying to relax . . . I mean, that's what I'm here to do. These obstacles that are placed in my mind, and in front of my fuckin' vision—I mean, they are not to be believed. You think it's easy, just doing the moment to moment . . . Just going from here to there, with maybe a little success thrown into the routine. And then to wind down when the opportunity presents itself. One would like to do as such. But . . . I mean, this and that— And then vice versa . . . How much can a society, not to mention an individual, endure. Maybe a little less permissiveness, on the societal front. Maybe a little less acceptance of those ill-fitting features. Maybe a little less quiet on certain issues, and a little more from the trumpets. Nothing wrong with that. Nothing wrong to speak out, when something makes you flinch.

PATSY. But all this is an abnormal response. So what, already?

VINNIE. What exactly are you saying, Patsy? I detect a note of something less than perfect pitch. Come clean here, please . . .

PATSY. I'm saying nothing, but what I'm thinking is— No one else in the club gives it a second thought or glance. From behind these closed doors, you find it so highly objectionable— That one has to wonder why? From a clinical point of view, Vinnie.

VINNIE. From a clinical point of view, Vinnie . . . From a clinical point of view? You fuckin'

flea market pimp— From a clinical point of view? Has the
pussy gone to your brain? You get laid once or twice, it
suddenly gives you the equivalence of a Ph.D.? I don't
want a unicorn in the locker room, and that makes me
what? That makes me crazy? Then suddenly my values are
to be questioned? No, I don't think so. Now I question
your values. And now I question the values in the fine
print. And now from this point on, I'm forced to read
between the lines, and then check between the cracks, and
sniff the sheets of every bed I ever lay down in . . . From
a clinical point of view, this is what I'm now forced to do.
And it has nothing to do with relaxation, or lack of. You
want to check into my head— You want to look for signs
of what might have been, what still could be?
Fine . . . That's okay. Meanwhile, I still deal with what
is. This is what I deal with, Patsy . . . What it is, and
what it is only.

Now you breathe deeply, okay? You try to relax a little.
I'm goin' to get dressed.

(VINNIE exits, leaving PATSY behind.
From the offstage locker room area we hear:)

VINNIE'S VOICE. What are you looking at, sister?

Scene 17

LORRAINE and RITA lounging in their apartment.
LORRAINE is wearing a nightgown, and cleaning a
hunting rifle.

LORRAINE. It was highly romantic . . . A small diner, right off the Interstate. I was sitting in the corner booth, drinking coffee, picking at some hash browns . . . There was a tiny jukebox on the table. Peter Lemongello was crooning softly.

I glanced out the window and saw a black sedan pull up. On the rooftop, a huge buck was strapped down— Fresh blood was still dripping from the corner of its mouth. The driver's door opened up, and he slid out of the car. He glanced towards the diner, and made eye contact with me through the glass. He smiled seductively, and then ran his filthy hand through his hair.

Although we had never talked, I felt completely at ease with him. I got up from my seat, and met him at the front door. He somehow knew I was going to be waiting for him . . . I suggested we go back to my motel room, and make mad passionate love. He didn't want to wait. He had to have me right then— This I could tell by the look in his one good eye; the other eye I could tell, was fake.

That didn't matter to me, though . . . We got into the back seat of his car, and he unsnapped my jeans. The buck's head was hanging over the side of the roof, and he appeared to be watching everything. The whole thing took less than a minute, but I was completely satisfied.

I left the car and headed back inside the diner—Suddenly I was hungry. Peter Lemongello was still singing the same song. My lover came in, ordered coffee to go, got back in his car, and drove off . . . Perhaps forever.

If we never meet again, at least we'll always have our moment.

(*Pause.*) I went back into the woods afterwards, and bagged a couple of squirrels. One shot each. No wasted effort. A clean, quick kill.

(*Pause.*) So how was your weekend?

Scene 18

The bistro. VINNIE is sitting at a table, working the books. HE apparently spots Pipino, heading for the kitchen area.

VINNIE. (*Calling out.*) Hey, Pipino . . .
What's the good word?
What's happening?
Bueno. Yeah, yeah . . . Mucho bueno.
How's that wife of yours—?
You keeping her happy?
(*Gives him a hand signal.*) You still give it to her every night?
No kidding . . .
You married her young, right?
She's never been with any other man?
Just you, all these years?
You think that's fair, Padre?
I know she's your wife— But you married her at what . . . She was eleven years old?
Go 'head, start on those dishes. Yeah, go 'head . . .
You see, you can't do that to a woman.
They resent you, for the rest of their life.

You can't take a woman that young, never let her be
with no one else. It's not healthy. Emotionally.

You know what I'm saying?

Don't play stupid, alright? I mean, let's have a
conversation.

I'm trying to treat you like an equal.

Pipino, listen to me . . . I'm trying to save your
marriage.

You want your wife to be happy, no?

So this is what you got to do—

Before it's too late, you gotta give her some freedom.

Like a bird.

Never mind the pigeons. I'm talking about your wife.

You gotta let her be with someone else.

Just to get it out of her system . . .

Another man. For your wife . . .

It's good for her. She'll love you more.

Makes the marriage stronger.

Stronger marriage. Right . . .

You told me she's always asleep, anyways. Right?

Your wife—she sleeps when you . . .

When you fuck your wife—she sleeps right through it,
no?

Yeah, that's what you told me.

Then you see what I'm talking about, right?

Pipino? You see what I'm saying?

Everybody needs a change, now and then.

. . . Yeah, right.

Don't thank me. It's okay.

Listen . . . Your wife ever mention me?

. . . she talk about Señor Vinnie?

Yeah, Mr. Vinnie. She likes me, no?

Of course she likes me. Yeah, that's what I thought.
Maybe you'll have me over to the house, one day.
To your house. Yeah, casa . . . Right.
We're all family, here . . . Familio . . .
All of us—we're family.
Yeah, yeah . . . Alright, go finish the dishes.

Scene 19

*LORRAINE and RITA in the park. THEY are winding
down after a morning jog.*

LORRAINE. I mean, there are things that work and
things that do not . . . Situations that are meant to fail,
others that aren't, but do anyway, and that rare bounce that
comes up lucky, but in the end isn't even worth
mentioning twice. You have yourself that you can count
on— And there's really not much more you need or
deserve.

RITA. Are you talking about me, or just speaking
generally?

LORRAINE. I'm speaking generally about you, I'm
talking generally about me, I'm trying to be specific as
hell about the universe in general . . . Do you care to
play devil's advocate?

RITA. Patsy has asked me to marry him.

LORRAINE. That's part of what I'm talking
about . . . People are always asking for something—
Asking something of you, for you . . . I mean, is it all

so necessary? Okay, he's asking you to marry him— But what do you get in return?

RITA. I told him I would marry him. (*Pause.*) I said yes.

LORRAINE. The desperation in your eyes is haunting. Do you ever notice it? Can you see it?

RITA. Can't you be happy for me?

LORRAINE. I don't believe I can. I think that somewhere deep down in my soul, I'd like to be happy for you . . . I think I'd really like that. It's just that I can't.

RITA. I see.

LORRAINE. I'll still come to the ceremony . . . there's no rule that says I can't. Don't try to keep me away.

RITA. We haven't really discussed a ceremony.

LORRAINE. Well, I think you should. That's something that should be discussed.

RITA. I just wanted you to be the first to know.

LORRAINE. I've heard that line throughout history. And I really don't see it as being a special honor. You want me to be the first to know? But you yourself knew before me, and so did what's-his-name . . .

RITA. Patsy.

LORRAINE. Yes, Patsy.

RITA. I'm sorry you don't approve, Lorraine.

LORRAINE. This is what makes the world go round . . . Albeit, in a not-so-circuitous route. You can't force triangles into a square, you can't tug on Superman's cape, you can't spit into the wind, you can't pull the mask off the old Lone Ranger, and . . . Oh well, never mind—

Let's just not pretend that these things can actually be done. It's all fully documented in the annals of history—

Society as a whole just doesn't work. Far be it for me to convince you otherwise.

People who think they can isolate their little patches of bliss, from the rest of the world's decay, are quite foolish. They hold hands with one another, as the fires rage around them—Smiling through it all.

Not knowing how oblivious they are to the entire mess. Their hands are tied together, unable to help defend themselves against the flames . . . They end up being accomplices to their own demise.

RITA. (*Pause.*) I want you to know, Lorraine, that hanging out with you is not as much fun as it used to be.

Scene 20

The bistro. VINNIE is behind the bar, talking on the phone. PATSY is seated nearby, glancing through a newspaper.

VINNIE. (*On phone.*) I told him that . . . Yeah . . . Yeah, I told him that. Of course I told him that . . . (*Pause.*) I told you, I told him that.
Sure . . . Of course . . .
What's the matter with you?
Of course I told him. You don't think I told him that? Why wouldn't I tell him?
PATSY. (*Looking up from paper.*) Told him what?
VINNIE. (*To Patsy.*) I'll be right with you.
PATSY. No problem.

VINNIE. (*On phone.*) Alright . . . Listen, I've gotta go.

Yeah . . . I gotta go. I'll call you later.

Why wouldn't I call you later?

Don't you want me to call you later?

I said I'd call you later . . .

Sure . . . Of course.

PATSY. I'm getting married.

VINNIE. (*Nodding to Patsy; still on phone.*) Yes, I told him . . . That's right.

Yes . . . Yes . . . I've told him.

He knows I've told him. He didn't forget. No, no . . .

Okay. Fine . . . Right. So long, Mom. (*HE hangs up.*)

PATSY. I'm getting married, Vinnie.

VINNIE. You're getting married.

PATSY. Yes.

VINNIE. Alright.

PATSY. What do you think?

VINNIE. I think . . .

I think it's something that happens.

If it's going to happen, it's going to happen.

Nothing you can do to avoid it.

What can I say, huh?

(*Pause.*) So what else is new?

Scene 21

The municipal building, marriage bureau. RITA, dressed in white wedding gown and sneakers, nervously paces the

floor. SHE unwraps a candy bar and takes a bite.
Suddenly PATSY arrives on the scene. HE's very
informally dressed—T-shirt, sweat pants, and loafers,
sans socks.

PATSY. You look quite beautiful.

RITA. Thank you.

PATSY. (*Pause.*) How do I look?

RITA. You look alright. (*Pause.*) Couldn't you have
worn a suit?

PATSY. I just came from the flea market.

RITA. Oh.

PATSY. I didn't want to wear a suit at the flea market,
'cause it wouldn't have been comfortable. I gotta feel
comfortable when I'm working. Otherwise, I can't sell
shoes. Who's going to buy shoes from a salesman who's
not comfortable?

RITA. Oh.

PATSY. Then I was going to bring the suit with me—
You know, leave it in the car . . .

RITA. Yes.

PATSY. But I would've felt terrible, if they had broken
into the car and stolen the suit . . . You expect for them
to break in, maybe steal the radio— But if they steal the
suit, that can just really be upsetting. 'Cause then I've got
to visualize some junkie thief, walking the streets in my
suit. Who needs that, right?

RITA. Oh.

PATSY. Anyway, you look very beautiful . . . And
the Nike shoes go real nice with the dress.

RITA. (*Looking down at her feet.*) Oh . . . I just ran
over from the office. I've got my shoes in the bag.

PATSY. Leave 'em, leave 'em ... You look perfect the way you are. Believe me, I know shoes. The outfit works this way.

RITA. You sure?

PATSY. Absolutely ... (*Pause.*) Where's your mother?

RITA. She couldn't make it.

PATSY. Oh ... I was looking forward to meeting her.

RITA. Perhaps another time.

PATSY. Sure.

RITA. (*Pause.*) Where's your mother?

PATSY. Out of the country.

RITA. Oh.

PATSY. Didn't I tell you that?

RITA. No ...

PATSY. Oh well ...

(*VINNIE enters the room, wearing a tuxedo suit and holding a small camera.*)

VINNIE. There's no place to park in this neighborhood ... I've been circling for an hour. Finally I found a meter. (*Checks his watch.*) I've got about fifteen minutes left. (*To Rita.*) Where's your mother?

PATSY. She couldn't make it.

VINNIE. (*An aside.*) How do you like that?

RITA. (*To Vinnie.*) That was very nice of you to dress so formally.

VINNIE. Hey, what can I say? It's an occasion. (*To Patsy.*) Where's your jacket?

PATSY. I came straight from the flea market.

VINNIE. (*Takes off his jacket, and hands it to Patsy.*) Here . . . You wear this.

PATSY. You sure?

VINNIE. Yeah, no problem. Put it on.

PATSY. (*Putting it on.*) Fits good.

VINNIE. Sure . . . One size fits all. (*To Rita.*) And don't you look lovely? (*Pause. To Patsy.*) What's with the kicks?

PATSY. Her shoes?

VINNIE. Yeah.

PATSY. You don't like 'em? I thought they go good with the dress.

VINNIE. (*To Patsy.*) A little too woodsy for my taste— Gives it that Kentucky shotgun flavor . . . Know what I mean?

RITA. I brought shoes . . . They're in my bag.

VINNIE. So there's no problem.

(*RITA takes the shoes from her bag and holds them up for all to see.*)

VINNIE. (*Not thrilled.*) Alright, maybe the sneakers aren't so bad.

PATSY. That's what I thought.

VINNIE. Sure, why not . . .

(*RITA, slightly confused, puts her shoes back in the bag. LORRAINE comes storming into the room.*)

LORRAINE. Am I too late?

RITA. Lorraine! I'm so glad you came.

LORRAINE. Did it happen yet? Have I missed it?

RITA. No, not yet.

(*LORRAINE glances over at Vinnie, and does a double take.*)

LORRAINE. (*To Rita.*) Which one of these is your intended?

RITA. (*Pointing to Patsy.*) This is Patsy . . .

VINNIE. (*To Lorraine.*) Haven't we met?

LORRAINE. No, never.

RITA. (*To Lorraine.*) This is Patsy's friend, Vinnie.

LORRAINE. (*To Vinnie.*) Please don't come near me.

RITA. (*To Vinnie.*) She's a little high-strung.

VINNIE. (*Shrugging it off.*) These things happen . . . She should probably cut down on the caffeine. Stuff does wild things to the head.

PATSY. Well, we should probably go inside . . .

RITA. Yes, I guess we should.

VINNIE. (*Holding up the camera.*) Alright, one quick shot.

(*VINNIE focuses in on the couple-to-be. Suddenly LORRAINE whips a hand gun from her purse. SHE grabs Rita by the neck and pulls her close. Then SHE points the gun at both Patsy and Vinnie.*)

RITA. Lorraine! What are you doing?!

LORRAINE. I'm saving you from the path of destruction.

PATSY. Hey, what the hell is going on?!

LORRAINE. (*To Patsy and Vinnie.*) Alright . . . You two get on the floor.

VINNIE. Hey, sweetheart . . . So you're a little upset. Come on, we'll let you kiss the bride.

LORRAINE. (*Firing a shot at their feet.*) I said, get on the floor!

(PATSY and VINNIE immediately hit the floor, face first.)

RITA. Oh, Patsy . . . I'm so sorry.

LORRAINE. (*To Vinnie and Patsy.*) Put your hands on top of your heads!

(THEY do as bid.)

VINNIE. (*To Patsy.*) I feel like I'm back in gym class.

PATSY. Please don't shoot us!

LORRAINE. Okay, I 'm leaving with the bride . . . Don't anybody move! If I see you following us, I'll kill us all.

VINNIE. Do me a favor . . . On the way out, drop a coin in my meter. It's the red T-Bird on the corner.

(LORRAINE quickly hustles RITA out of the room. PATSY and VINNIE are left on the floor, hands on head.)

VINNIE. (*Pause; to Patsy.*) Can I assume there's not going to be a reception?

END OF ACT I

ACT II

Scene 22

LORRAINE sitting in a jailhouse holding cell. SHE yells out to whomever might be listening.

LORRAINE. Guard!!! Guard!
I'd like to make a phone call!
A phone call, please . . .
I have a right to call my therapist!
Who did I kill? Did I kill somebody?
All I did was stop a wedding! I'm a political prisoner, here . . . It was an act of loyalty, of friendship, of love . . . How does one get tossed in jail for an act of love? (*To self.*) This sucks . . .

Scene 23

RITA sitting with LORRAINE in her apartment.

RITA. Are you okay?
LORRAINE. Yes, I'm quite fine . . . Thank you for bailing me out.
RITA. Would you like some tea?
LORRAINE. No, thank you.
RITA. (*Pause.*) So . . . What are your plans?

LORRAINE. I'm thinking of joining the Peace Corps—

What do you mean, "what are your plans?"

RITA. I was just wondering . . .

LORRAINE. . . . whether I was a danger to society?

RITA. No, I didn't mean that.

LORRAINE. Yes you did.

RITA. No I didn't.

LORRAINE. I believe you did.

RITA. Honestly, I did not.

LORRAINE. My gut reaction is that you did . . . I have to go with my inner feeling.

RITA. For God's sake, Lorraine . . . I didn't mean that.

LORRAINE. Yes you did!!!

That's what you meant, you fuckin', lying whore bitch! Admit it!!! Admit it!!!

The truth will set you free!

Say it . . . Tell the world . . .

You can't go on living a lie.

Speak to Jesus! Let him hear you!

He is ready . . .

RITA. Speak to Jesus?

LORRAINE. Okay, I got a little carried away. Never mind. (*Pause.*) What are your plans for tonight?

RITA. My plans?

What are my plans for tonight?

LORRAINE. While I was sitting in the joint, there was some singing coming from the adjoining cell— Four Young Black Men . . .

They were very good.

"Because under township guidelines, these charges are classified as only a misdemeanor, police have enlisted the help of world-famous animal hypnotist, Roberto LaFlembeur—in the hope that he can somehow teach the dogs to speak. If that can be accomplished, authorities would take sworn statements from each of the dogs, in an attempt to convict Lettera of a higher charge.

"When taken into custody for booking, Lettera would only say, 'Why don't you just ask them if they were satisfied.' " (*VINNIE puts down the paper, and looks over at Patsy. Pause.*) The universal question . . .

Scene 25

PATSY and RITA in Patsy's apartment. The morning. THEY are getting dressed.

PATSY. What time did you get in last night?
RITA. About midnight.
You were sound asleep.
PATSY. No I wasn't . . .
I heard you come in.
RITA. Then why are you asking what time I got in?
PATSY. I was awake . . . I just didn't know the time.
RITA. I see.
PATSY. (*Pause.*) Actually, you fell asleep kind of
RITA. I was very tired.
PATSY. Did you have a good time?
RITA. It was okay.

They were also waiting to get bailed out, and happened to mention they were performing tonight—a small club on the fringes of gentrification. Would you like to go hear them?
RITA. Four young black men were singing in jail, and invited you to their club date?
LORRAINE. Four Young Black Men . . . That's the name of the group.
RITA. Oh . . .
LORRAINE. Would you like to come?
RITA. I don't think I can.
LORRAINE. Are you getting married tonight?
RITA. No . . .
LORRAINE. Then what's the problem? . . . Would you feel uncomfortable around the brothers?
RITA. What brothers?
LORRAINE. Four Young Black Men . . .
RITA. No, that's not it . . . Don't forget, I love soul music. I have all of the Diana Ross albums.
LORRAINE. Please don't patronize me, here . . .
RITA. I'm not.
LORRAINE. You don't have to treat me with kid gloves.
RITA. I didn't think I was.
LORRAINE. Your attitude is slightly holier than thou.
RITA. What are you talking about? You're the one who acts insane, and I have an attitude problem?
LORRAINE. I am not insane.
RITA. I said, "acts insane."
I did not say you were insane.
(*Pause.*) Who are we kidding here?
Lorraine, you are insane.

You are as crazy as a bedbug...

You would be deemed certifiable, by the highest court of insanity in the land— You would be judged incapable of making correct decisions, determining right from wrong, good from bad, night from day...

The truth is, you shouldn't be allowed to handle your own affairs, not to mention commenting on the affairs of others... My God! If it were up to me, I wouldn't even let you butter your own toast, feed the fish, or open junk mail... You're my friend, and I love you—But you're a fuckin' crackpot. And it used to be cute, and funny, and amusing— But it's not anymore. You understand what I'm. saying here? It's a deal gone sour. No one is laughing anymore. You understand?

LORRAINE. And perhaps someone like you— The girl next door, who wears a white wedding gown with running shoes... Who goes down to the local courthouse, with the intention of marrying a flea market shoe pimp named Patsy... Perhaps you're the proper authority to monitor my behavior. You're the right choice, to help me stay the straight and narrow.

(There is a long pause. THEY BOTH stare at each other, waiting for the next move.)

RITA. Alright... I will go with you to hear "Four Young Black Men."

Is that what this is all about?

That's what you want to hear, right?

Yes, I will go with you.

LORRAINE. *(Suddenly changing face.)* You will?

RITA. Yes.

LORRAINE. You'll have a great time, Rita.

You've got to hear them— They're outta sight.

Listen, maybe we'll grab a bite to eat afterwards, huh? There's a new Creole place downtown everyone's talking about.

This is superb. Are you psyched?

I am... Just like the old days, right?

RITA. Sure.

LORRAINE. I'm going to take a shower... Be re in a minute.

(SHE jumps up and heads off to the bathroom. R on the couch, biting her lip.)

Scene 24

The Bistro. VINNIE reads to Patsy from a

VINNIE. *(Reading aloud.)* "Townshi morning arrested a forty-year-old truck having sexual relations with twenty Lettera was arrested after local A' police off.

"According to Judy Denr employee... Mr. Lettera had shelter, each time adopting a l were raised when Mr. Letter and returned another dog pregnant.

PATSY. Were you drunk?

RITA. No . . . I had one glass of wine.

PATSY. Oh . . .

I was a little horny last night.

RITA. (*Looking through her purse.*) Have you seen my keys?

PATSY. I thought perhaps we were . . .

RITA. You thought what?

PATSY. I thought that we were going to fool around—

You know, when you got home.

I was sort of looking forward to it.

RITA. Fool around?

What the hell does that mean—?

Play with blocks?

Can't you come out and say exactly what you mean?

PATSY. It was implied earlier in the evening. The body language, the incidental contact, the look in your eyes . . . I was supposed to get a piece of tookie, last night.

RITA. A piece of tookie?

I feel like I'm watching "Sesame Street."

PATSY. I don't understand what game you're playing—

You can't treat someone like that.

We were supposed to spend the evening together; fine, you went off with Lorraine . . . The point that she should be locked up for life, is a moot point, apparently. Let's put that aside for a moment.

I was waiting to be with you. You know that. If you're not too tired to go out and listen to some singing convicts— How can you be too tired to give yourself to the man you love? Didn't you hear me whispering in your ear?

RITA. No . . . What were you saying?

PATSY. It doesn't matter what I was saying—That's not the point.

I was supposed to get laid last night.

I was waiting for it all night.

You can't make someone wait all night, and then turn your back on him . . . That's the shittiest thing in the world to do.

RITA. Tell me what you were whispering, Patsy.

PATSY. I don't remember what I was whispering . . . What's the difference, you were out like a light. I was so wound up, I couldn't sleep. Had to go into the bathroom, and jerk off into the sink.

RITA. Were you thinking of me?

PATSY. Huh?

RITA. Were you thinking of me, when you were in the bathroom?

PATSY. No . . . I wouldn't give you that satisfaction.

RITA. Oh. (*Pause.*) That's too bad.

PATSY. I lied.

Yes, I was thinking of you.

RITA. That excites me.

PATSY. Does it?

RITA. Yes . . . Into the sink?

PATSY. Yes.

RITA. While I was sleeping?

PATSY. Yes.

RITA. And then what happened?

PATSY. I wiped myself off . . .

RITA. Yes.

PATSY. . . . on your stockings.

RITA. You used my stockings, to wipe yourself off?
PATSY. Yes.
RITA. The ones I've just put on?
PATSY. They look familiar.
RITA. (*Takes them off.*) That's disgusting.
PATSY. I don't think it was a conscious thing.
RITA. It wasn't a conscious thing? . . .
Wiping your ding-a-ling with my stockings?
PATSY. The room was dark.
RITA. Oh, please . . .
PATSY. A moment ago you were excited.
RITA. Isn't it amazing how quickly things can change?

Scene 26

LORRAINE at her therapist's office. SHE is lying on the couch.

LORRAINE. I'd like to try a little experiment here . . . Maybe turn the tables a wee bit. What I'd like to do, is hear what you have to say. Out of curiosity, I'd be fascinated to see if you have anything to add to this . . . Or to that . . . Or to anything, I suppose.
Anything at all . . .
Because, I don't particularly have anything to say to you right now. At least, nothing you'd be interested in hearing. Things are just going along swimmingly. I feel on top of all situations, in control, able to slide gracefully from moment to moment.

And, of course, God bless your heart—I haven't forgotten that you failed to return my jailhouse calls.

Your beeper was on the blink? I see . . .

My checkbook will be on the blink, next time your bill comes.

(*Pause.*) Okay . . . So how about it? Just talk—I'm really a very good listener; just a little out of practice. Give me a shot.

Let's hear what's on your mind, pal . . .

Come on, I'm waiting.

Scene 27

The bistro. VINNIE is having a drink, alone.

VINNIE. (*Apparently spotting someone.*) Pipino? . . . That you?

What are you doin', sneaking around?

Sneaking around . . .

Never mind.

(*Pause.*) Come on over. Sit down. Have a drink.

Cerveza? . . . Rum? . . .

Why not? What's the rush?

Where the fuck you running to?

All these years you been married— And you still run home to the wife.

Yeah, yeah . . . I know. It's like a disease.

You can't never get rid of it.

Stop babbling for a second. That's a bad habit, Pipino. You can't talk through someone . . . You wait till he's finished, and then you talk. Understand what I'm saying here?

Yeah, comprendo . . .

Now you made me lose my thought process—

What was I saying? Oh, yeah . . .

Patsy is the same as you, now.

He runs home quick. To be with his girl . . .

Yeah, Patsy got a girl.

She's got him running like crazy.

Yeah, loco. Crazy, right.

But this is a vicious cycle, Pipino. It's a dead-end setup. Eventually it gets you. In the long run, forget about it. You can't beat this type of trap. 'Cause that's what it is— it's a trap. You end up running here, running there, and finally you end up like a chicken without a head.

Chicken . . . No, no . . . I ate already. That's not what I'm saying here.

Forget it. It's late already . . . Go home to the wife, Pipino.

She's probably layin' there, waiting for you to pounce.

Hey, at least it gives you something to think about, on the way home.

Your wife? . . . Your wife, what?

Did she really? She told you to say hello, to me? No kidding?

Mr. Vinnie, huh? That's nice—Real nice.

(*Pause.*) How did she say it? I mean, was it just in passing—or did she say it like she meant it? Was she sincere, Pipino?

Sincerity means the world to me.

It's important. It separates the real ones from the frauds.

Frauds. Phonies . . . Fakes . . .

When you smile like that, it means you don't understand a thing I'm saying.

Yeah, yeah . . . Comprendo.

Go 'head, Pipino . . . I'll lock up in a minute.

Good night to you too . . . (*VINNIE sits there, alone with his thoughts.*)

Scene 28

PATSY and RITA at Patsy's apartment.

PATSY. Who stinks? . . .

I stink?

RITA. It's not the end of the world—

Your breath is bad, that's all. You have bad breath at this moment.

PATSY. Why don't you just say what's really on your mind, Rita . . . ?

Let's stop playing these childish games.

Enough with the masquerading of feelings.

Enough with the camouflaging of your soul . . . Okay?

People can't be mind readers. I can't guess about words you never let me hear.

Now, really . . . What is it?

RITA. Your breath stinks.

Really, that's it in a nutshell.

PATSY. Your mother.

RITA. I beg your pardon?

PATSY. What's the matter, you deaf? I said, "Your mother."

RITA. What about my mother?

PATSY. What about your mother?

RITA. Yes . . . What about my mother, Patsy?

PATSY. (*Not really sure.*) Your mother's breath stinks. It stinks to high hell.

A fuckin' fire battalion couldn't put out the stink from your mother's mouth.

RITA. You've never met my mother.

PATSY. And now you know why.

RITA. And now I know why? . . .

You imbecile.

How do you know what my mother smells like, if you've never even met her?

PATSY. You don't think I hear things?

It's a small world.

People talk . . .

Things get around.

Everyone knows about your mother.

RITA. I have met some immature people in my life— but never anyone like you. I happen to mention that your breath stinks, a public service type of gratuity— And instead of thanking me, so as not to go out into public, unaware of the disaster at hand . . . You become so thrown, so embarrassed, that you have to revert to a childish game of name calling. And believe me, mister, if you want to stoop to that level—you are fooling with the wrong person. I'll make you so small, you'll have to look up to look down.

PATSY. Oh, yeah?

RITA. That's right, needle dick.

PATSY. Needle dick? . . .

Who are you calling needle dick?

RITA. Let me amend that . . .

Dragon breath, needle dick.

PATSY. (*Beside himself.*) How 'bout you?

RITA. What about me?

PATSY. Just don't get me started.

RITA. Started on what?

Go ahead, make something up.

PATSY. I don't have to make something up. (*Pause.*)
Fishwife.

RITA. Fishwife? . . . What's that supposed to mean?

PATSY. You know what it means.

RITA. What does it mean, short-on?

PATSY. Sleeping with you is like sleeping with a
corpse. You might as well be dead. Doesn't passion mean
anything to you?

RITA. Maybe if I was sleeping with a real man, I
wouldn't have that problem.

PATSY. So you admit it!

RITA. So you admit it!!!

PATSY. You're a bull dyke . . . Come on, you can
tell me the truth.

RITA. Sorry, breakfast-sausage penis . . . You don't
get off the hook that easily. Don't look for lies to cover up
your inadequacies. I know it would be easier that way, but
that's just not the way it is.

PATSY. I wasn't so inadequate when you wanted to get
married . . . When you wanted to have a child?

RITA. I guess we all make mistakes, huh?

PATSY. Yeah, well, I guess so.

And the truth be known, I never thought you were a quality person. You have very definite character deficiencies . . . Basically you are undeserving of true love, true happiness. You are destined for a lifetime of bitterness— I just want to warn you now. Because I was willing to help you change, help you become complete as an individual, as a contributing factor in this universe. But now I think it's just not worth the effort. I don't think the returns are going to be worthwhile.

I'm sorry, Rita. You just don't measure up.

RITA. I'm sorry if I hurt your feelings.

PATSY. Negatory on that count, my dear . . . Sticks and stones, you know. What I'm sorry about is, you felt the need to take that route— It might have been much easier just to speak the truth.

RITA. You're a pompous fool, aren't you?

PATSY. I don't know . . . But I would've been willing to talk about it.

RITA. I'm sure.

PATSY. And now if you'd excuse me, I'd like to get on with my life.

RITA. What exactly are you asking me?

PATSY. I'm asking you to get the hell out.

RITA. (*Gathering up a few things.*) I was planning to do that.

(*PATSY reaches for a bottle of mouthwash, takes a hit, gargles right there in the room, and swallows it down.*)

PATSY. Okay? . . . I've fixed my life, let's see you fix yours.

RITA. (*Heading out.*) You're an asshole.

PATSY. Your mother.
RITA. (*Wheeling around.*) Your mother!!!
And your father, and your dead grandparents!!

(*PATSY moves towards her. HE grabs her by the arms, and pulls her close. Passionately, HE kisses her on the mouth . . . long and hard. RITA staggers back, dazed and confused.*)

PATSY. (*Starting to unsnap his pants.*) I need you, now!

(*RITA gives him a bewildered look, before turning and exiting. PATSY is left alone, staring at the door as RITA leaves.*)

Scene 29

VINNIE and PATSY after hours at the bistro. PATSY seems to be quite heartbroken.

VINNIE. Patsy, listen to me now . . .
Hear me clearly on this one issue— The thing you must understand . . . The paramount point to be made here is that we're talking two different breeds here.
Okay?
Apples and oranges, oil and water, Sonny and Cher . . .

They are different than us. Women are different. You're gonna sit there, rack your brain looking for a solution that doesn't exist?

There is no answer to the madness. And that's the key.

Understand that they can't be solved, can't be decoded—

Understand that yes means no, no means maybe, and stay means go . . . Understand all that, maintain a sense of dignity, and smile through it all and you've won.

PATSY. What do I win?

VINNIE. You get to play another round. One more spin on the Ferris wheel, before you're forced to jump off . . . If you're lucky, you won't be too far from the ground. If not, better have a parachute.

What do you want to do, rewrite the rules? You can't, because there are none. You want to have some order to the madness? You can't have that, because the inmates are running the asylum.

One day at a time, Pats . . . That's how this game is played. No rules, no logic, ultimately no winner declared. Just be standing when the bell rings. Really, that's all there is.

Scene 30

LORRAINE and RITA. In the park.

LORRAINE. Are you sad?

RITA. No.

LORRAINE. Do you blame yourself for the failure of this relationship?

RITA. No, not really . . .
Would it be alright if I blamed you?
LORRAINE. Yes, perfectly.
RITA. You're not a very nice person, are you, Lorraine?
LORRAINE. I'm troubled.
RITA. You're not troubled—
You're just not very nice.
LORRAINE. I'm really not to blame here, Rita.
RITA. No, you're right.
LORRAINE. I suppose this wouldn't be a very good time to tell you that I'm sexually attracted to you . . . That I have been for many years, now. I would like to sleep with you, but not at the risk of damaging our friendship.
RITA. I believe our friendship is fairly damaged already.
LORRAINE. So you do want to have sex?
RITA. No.
LORRAINE. If it means anything to you, I don't believe I'm a lesbian. It's just something that I need to get out of my system.
RITA. That's very comforting.
LORRAINE. You'll think about it?
RITA. No, I won't think about it. Okay? . . . I won't think about it. Now please, you think about me not thinking about it.
Can you do that, Lorraine?
LORRAINE. I suppose so.
RITA. Thank you.
LORRAINE. I just want you to know, I'll be there for you. Whatever you need from me, I will give you. Has anyone ever said that to you before?
RITA. My mother.
LORRAINE. Oh.

Scene 31

PATSY and RITA, the final go-round. SHE is removing several final items from his apartment.

PATSY. I just want this to end, with one final, parting thought: that as a human being, as a breathing, living creature—you are severely lacking.

You are lacking in the fundamental areas of character, morality, loyalty, and common sense. You will lead the remaining years of your existence traveling in blind circles, unaware of the repetition of your search. Along the way, you will bore the same people endlessly, and to such a degree, that they will shudder at the thought of your returning . . . Happiness will elude you, as will any sort of personal sanity. I pity you greatly, and I pray for society. I suggest you do so as well.

RITA. And may I just add that you will spend the rest of your years jacking off into sinks . . . Because no woman will be able to stand the sight or smell of you. If you're lucky, some bathroom manufacturer will hire you as their national spokesman— A testament to the wear and tear their sinks can endure. (*Pause.*) You are a pitiful penis porcelain pounder . . .

PATSY. (*Watching her take a leather bag.*) That's my leather bag, you klepto whore!

RITA. It's not your bag . . . You stole it from an old lady at the flea market. I'm just returning it to her.

PATSY. You are a disease waiting to be named.

RITA. (*Heading for the door.*) Your mother! (*SHE quickly exits the apartment, slamming the door behind her.*)

PATSY. (*Runs to the door, opens it. Pause; calling out.*) Remember when I told you what a great cook you were? I lied!!! You can't cook for shit!!! (*Satisfied, HE slams the door and stalks out of the room.*)

Scene 32

VINNIE and PATSY at the bistro. THEY are looking at the new waitress.

PATSY. So who's that?

VINNIE. Where?

PATSY. The new one.

VINNIE. The new waitress?

PATSY. Yeah.

VINNIE. Christine . . .

PATSY. Christine, huh?

VINNIE. The blonde?

PATSY. Is it natural?

VINNIE. I'm working on that.

PATSY. You've made the old move already, say hey?

VINNIE. I'm testing the waters.

PATSY. With Christine, huh?

VINNIE. (*Nodding in her direction.*) This one right over here . . .

PATSY. That's Christine.

VINNIE. Or Maria, or Constance . . .

PATSY. So what you're saying is . . .

VINNIE. What's in a name, right?

PATSY. And those waters are being tested?

VINNIE. Does a bear shit in the woods?

PATSY. I hear you.

VINNIE. Of course you do.

PATSY. Loud and clear.

VINNIE. I'm on the warpath.

PATSY. Take no prisoners.

VINNIE. That's the only way to play.

PATSY. (*Pause.*) She's very sexy, isn't she?

VINNIE. She's okay.

PATSY. I love her neck.

VINNIE. Her neck?

PATSY. I really like her ears, too.

VINNIE. Her ears?

PATSY. Like the most delicate of noodles . . . Little semolina noodles. I'd give anything, just to sprinkle a bit of Parmesan cheese right on the tip there—

VINNIE. And then perhaps a nibble on the lobe area?

PATSY. Exactly.

VINNIE. So can we assume you're an ear man?

PATSY. I would say basically, yes . . . Except of course, when you're dealing with a face like that.

VINNIE. She does have a magnificent face, doesn't she?

PATSY. It should be hanging on a flag.

VINNIE. Wonderfully structured— Perfect bone alignment.

PATSY. Not to mention that ass . . .

VINNIE. I didn't even want to bring it up.

PATSY. And you've already started the ball rolling, huh? The wheels are in motion? She knows you're here?

VINNIE. Yes, negotiations have begun . . . Why?

PATSY. Well, I would just like to know. I would like to be sure, because obviously my interest has been piqued here . . . This is a situation I would ordinarily pursue. My fancy has been tickled, and my romantic senses have been aroused.

VINNIE. Makes you feel alive, doesn't it? This is a very natural response.

PATSY. I just don't want you to feel . . .

VINNIE. Please, please . . .

These are basic tribal laws.

As old as the sun and stars.

What do you want to do—deny? . . .

You want to deny the most primitive of urges?

You want to repress the savage instinct?

Why, as a friend, would I want that?

And what kind of friend would I be?

PATSY. Thank you. That's very kind. Very understanding.

VINNIE. There is nothing wrong in looking, in perhaps making a passing comment, or in receiving some kind of vicarious pleasure. If my love life makes you a happier person, then why not? Am I right?

PATSY. So just to clear the issue here—

You've established the origins for some sort of romantic web . . . Tangled as it may be.

You know it, she knows it. Perhaps without documentation, without the exact words . . . But the seed has been planted here; and the two of you know where the next steps will be taken. Some forsaken fruit is about to be peeled. Is that the case? I should probably know, so I can get on with my life.

VINNIE. Because otherwise?

PATSY. Because otherwise, I would like to act on those primal urges. I would like to dive into the deepest of uncharted depths, and see what creatures lurk beyond the lagoon. These are things I'd like to try, because my biological time bomb is just about ready to blow . . . Tick, tick, tick, Vinnie. And I think you know what I mean.

VINNIE. I understand what you're saying—And I appreciate the honesty.

PATSY. I knew that you would.

VINNIE. There is, however, the slightest of problems here.

PATSY. And that is?

VINNIE. I believe the young woman in question may already be involved.

PATSY. You're kidding.

VINNIE. It's just a feeling . . .

PATSY. Just a feeling.

VINNIE. Yes . . .

PATSY. What gives you the impression?

VINNIE. She told me so.

PATSY. Oh.

VINNIE. Can you believe that?

PATSY. I'm not sure.

VINNIE. I mean, is this a cockteaser, or wha'?

PATSY. I'm not sure.

VINNIE. We hadn't even been introduced yet, and those were the first words out of her mouth.

PATSY. That she was involved . . .

VINNIE. Yeah . . .

That's all I needed to hear.

I immediately became primed for action.
PATSY. It became a challenge?
VINNIE. It became an obsession.
PATSY. Be careful, Vinnie.
VINNIE. Please, my friend . . .
I don't play these games with my heart.
After all, that's the key.
PATSY. So what's the game plan?
VINNIE. The game plan?
PATSY. What do you do next?
VINNIE. I just wait it out . . .
She gets off in five minutes.
And then, watch me in action.
PATSY. The fur is ready to fly, huh?
VINNIE. Like taking candy from a baby.
PATSY. You feel good about it, huh?
VINNIE. You have to . . .
You can't start any other way.
PATSY. I admire that, Vinnie.
It's a hell of a way to live your life.
VINNIE. (*Watching her.*) She's coming out now . . .
PATSY. What are you going to say?
VINNIE. I have no script.
I just have to be me.
PATSY. Go head.
VINNIE. (*To self.*) Come on over, sweetheart . . .
Come say hello to the Vin man.
PATSY. She seems to be lingering near the kitchen
doors.
VINNIE. Just a little cat-and-mouse game, Pats . . .
Watch and learn. Never too old to pick up some tips.
PATSY. She's touching her makeup.
VINNIE. That's alright . . . She doesn't know yet
that I'm a natural type of guy. Give her time, she'll learn.
PATSY. She's going into the kitchen . . .

VINNIE. That's alright.

PATSY. Now she's coming out of the kitchen.

VINNIE. That's alright.

PATSY. And she's not alone.

VINNIE. (*Pause.*) That's alright . . .
Who's she with?

PATSY. Pipino.

VINNIE. That's alright.

PATSY. She's kissing him.
She's kissing Pipino . . .

VINNIE. She is, isn't she?

PATSY. And he's kissing her.
It seems to be mutual.

VINNIE. It does, doesn't it?

PATSY. They're leaving . . .

VINNIE. They are, aren't they?

PATSY. And Pipino is waving to us . . . (*PATSY waves to Pipino.*)

VINNIE. (*Calling out.*) Hey, Pipino!!!
How's the missus?

(VINNIE and PATSY watch them exit the premises.)

PATSY. They've gone . . .
She left with Pipino.
Pipino the dishwasher.
Pipino the illegal alien dishwasher . . .
With a wife and twelve kids . . .
(*Pause.*) What an understanding wife he has.

VINNIE. She wasn't so great-looking, anyway . . .

PATSY. The waitress?

VINNIE. The ex-waitress . . .
When she comes in tomorrow, tell her she's fired.

PATSY. Okay.

VINNIE. Just a business decision.

PATSY. I understand.

VINNIE. You gotta be able to do the job.

An honest day's work, for a day's pay.

PATSY. That's right.

VINNIE. I watched her with the customers—

They don't connect with her . . . There's no chemistry there. You have to establish a relationship with the table; you know that.

PATSY. I know that.

VINNIE. She didn't know the menu, either . . . How you goin' to answer the questions, if you don't know the menu?

PATSY. You can't.

VINNIE. 'Course not . . .

She was also a thief.

PATSY. No.

VINNIE. The girl has a problem, my friend.

PATSY. She was stealing?

VINNIE. Wouldn't write up the bill, pocket the cash . . . Now and then, more often than not.

PATSY. And you kept her on?

VINNIE. I was trying to steer her into counseling.

She's a sick puppy.

PATSY. That's a shame.

VINNIE. Wiped out half the silverware . . .

All the good knives and forks.

PATSY. She'd dump it in the purse?

VINNIE. Right down her pants.

PATSY. Oh, my.

VINNIE. What are you gonna do, huh?

It's a sick world out there, Pats.

PATSY. Tell me about it.

VINNIE. I was thinking about pressing charges.

PATSY. You probably should have.

VINNIE. Lot of experts think so . . .

Tough Love, you know?
PATSY. You have to hurt them to help them.
VINNIE. But it's just not me.
PATSY. I guess not.
VINNIE. Whatever . . .
PATSY. Yeah.
VINNIE. (*Pause.*) Did I mention she was unsanitary?
PATSY. No, you didn't.
VINNIE. She could've bathed a little more often.
A little more thoroughly, perhaps.
PATSY. I understand . . .
No place for that in an eating establishment.
VINNIE. Water under the bridge.
PATSY. Yes, sir.

(Slowly the LIGHTS start to fade . . . .)

VINNIE. Yes, sir . . . Water under the bridge.

(As we go to BLACK, we hear the same Rock 'n Roll tune that began Act I." The song continues.)

THE END

COSTUME PLOT

Scene 1
PATSY: white short sleeved shirt, black twill pants, black belt, black tie shoes, watch with leather band, gold chain

VINNIE: black silk shirt, grey pleated pants, black Pierre Cardin belt, black slip on shoes, gold/black ring, jeweled watch, gold chain

Scene 2
LORRAINE: leather skirt, orange top, black pumps, black/gold earrings, black/blue sunglasses, rings, pantyhose, black/gold watch, black purse

RITA: blue skirt, grey pumps, grey belt, pearl earrings, pink headband, brown/ gold watch, pearl necklace

Scene 3
LORRAINE: Same
VINNIE: Same

Scene 4
PATSY: T-shirt, sneakers, gold chain
VINNIE: Same

Scene 5
PATSY: Same
RITA: jeans, black belt, blue/white T-shirt, white anklets, pearl earrings, pink headband, pearl necklace

Scene 6

VINNIE: change shirt to white striped silk shirt, all the rest remains the same

Scene 7

PATSY: nude briefs
RITA: purple dress, multicolored sash, underwear, brown suede shoes, pearl earrings, pearl necklace, pink headband

Scene 8

LORRAINE: jeans, sunglasses, yellow top, sneakers
RITA: Same

Scene 9

PATSY: cartoon T-shirt, jeans, sneakers, plaid shirt,
RITA: Same
VINNIE: black T-shirt, white jacket, jeans, brown snakeskin belt, grey pleated pants, black belt, black shoes, watch, ring, chain, sunglasses

Scene 10

PATSY: Same
LORRAINE: blue bathrobe, blue/yellow flip-flops, (over cream blouse, grey skirt.)

Scene 11

PATSY: remove plaid shirt add sunglasses
VINNIE: Possibly same if no jeans with snakeskin belt in previous scene, otherwise replace jeans with grey pleated pants w/black belt.

Scene 12

LORRAINE: cream blouse with attached tie (buttons in front), grey wool suit (or just skirt), black shoes, big pearl earrings, black/gold watch

Scene 13

RITA: big Van Gogh T-shirt, underpants
PATSY: boxer shorts, add jeans, sneakers, yellow long sleeved shirt

Scene 14

PATSY: Same
VINNIE: grey striped shirt, grey pleated pants, black shoes, assorted jewelry, black belt

Scene 15

RITA: patterned buttoned shirt, yellow leggings, yellow flip-flops, pearls
LORRAINE: hunting cap, combat jacket, combat pants, army belt, boots, olive T-shirt, dog tags, plastic watch, olive socks

Scene 16

PATSY: towel, flesh briefs
VINNIE: towel, flesh briefs

Scene 17

RITA: white flowered nightgown, yellow flip-flops
LORRAINE: yellow nightgown & negligee, yellow/blue flip-flops

Scene 18
VINNIE: Same as Scene 14

Scene 19
LORRAINE: black leggings, black jog top, pink/white sneakers, orange headband, yellow wristbands, orange socks, towel
RITA: running shorts, running top, white slouch socks, sneakers

Scene 20
VINNIE: Same except replace grey pants with tux pants
PATSY: navy sweatpants, sneakers, athletic T-shirt, chain

Scene 21
RITA: wedding gown, wedding veil, white slouch socks, sneakers, pearls
PATSY: T-shirt, navy sweatpants, sneakers, chain
VINNIE: tux jacket & pants, cummerbund, black bow tie, tux shirt, black shoes, black socks, dry assorted jewelry
LORRAINE: yellow silk blouse, blue skirt, blue pumps, pearl earrings, watch, black purse

Scene 22
LORRAINE: Same without jewelry and purse

Scene 23
LORRAINE: Same
RITA: pink top, jeans, suede shoes, pearls

Scene 24

PATSY: jeans, sneakers, T-shirt, chain

VINNIE: grey pleated pants, grey silk shirt, black belt, black shoes, assorted jewelry

Scene 25

RITA: peach skirt, blue flowered blouse, beige belt, beige pumps, pantyhose, pearls

PATSY: sneakers, jeans, grey socks, chain, striped white/lavender T-shirt

Scene 26

LORRAINE: grey wool skirt, black pumps, maroon blouse, pearl earrings

Scene 27

VINNIE: Same

Scene 28

PATSY: jeans, T-shirt, sneakers, chain

RITA: jeans, blue top, pearls, brown shoulder bag, black belt, brown suede shoes

Scene 29

PATSY: Same
VINNIE: Same

Scene 30

RITA: Replace top with striped silk blouse

LORRAINE: black pumps, patterned dress, black purse, gold earrings, watch

Scene 31

RITA: Same but add brown bag

PATSY: colored button-down shirt, jeans, sneakers, chain

Scene 32

PATSY: Same
VINNIE: Same

PROPERTY LIST

Chivas bottle
Whiskey bottle
2 Shot glasses
Art exhibit program
Purse
Laundry basket w/
     sheets, towels, shirts
Supermarket basket w/
      milk, orange juice, eggs, bread (Rita)
      can of fruit, orange juice, bread (Patsy)
1 Line
1 Blanket/sheet
Sunglasses
Newspaper—*New York Post*
Hand gun
Suitcase w/shoes on stand
2 Lunch bags
Book (paperback) (Rita)
Boots/cap
2 White towels
Hunting rifle
Cloth to wipe rifle
Ledger book
1 towel (Lorraine)
Rotary telephone (black)
Leather bag with shoes inside
Bouquet of flowers
Camera
Bartender's rag
Bottle of mouthwash

1 Cardboard box with clothing
1 Table/2 chairs
1 White linen table cloth
2 White linen napkins
2 Cups with saucers holding cappuccino
1 bottle of liqueur with 2 little spoons
2 Sandwiches (Vinnie, Patsy)
1 Pickle
Popcorn
Yogurt
Coffee
Green apple

Set   List

Sculpture
Park bench
Bar
Barstool
Bed/sofa
Table with chairs
Folding table

TWO NEW COMEDIES FROM
━━━━━━ SAMUEL FRENCH, Inc.━━━━━━

FAST GIRLS. (Little Theatre). Comedy. Diana Amsterdam. 2m., 3f. Int. Lucy Lewis is a contemporary, single woman in her thirties with what used to be called a "healthy sex life," much to the chagrin of her mother, who feels Lucy is too fast, too easy—and too single. Her best friend, on the other hand, neighbor Abigail McBride, is deeply envious of Lucy's ease with men. When Lucy wants to date a man she just calls him up, whereas Abigail sits home alone waiting for Ernest, who may not even know she exists, to call. The only time Abigail isn't by the phone is after Lucy has had a hot date, when she comes over to Lucy's apartment to hear the juicy details and get green with envy. Sometimes, though, Lucy doesn't want to talk about it, which drives Abigail *nuts* ("If you don't tell me about men I have no love life!"). Lucy's mother arrives to take the bull by the horns, so to speak, arriving with a challenge. Mom claims no man will marry Lucy (even were she to *want to* get married), because she's too easy. Lucy takes up the challenge, announcing that she is going to get stalwart ex-boyfriend Sidney ("we're just friends") Epstein to propose to her. Easier said than done. Sidney doesn't *want* a fast girl. Maybe dear old Mom is right, thinks Lucy. Maybe fast girls *can't* have it all. "Amsterdam makes us laugh, listen and think."—Daily Record. "Brilliantly comic moments."—The Monitor. "rapidly paced comedy with a load of laughs . . . a funny entertainment with some pause for reflection on today's [sexual] confusion."—Suburban News. "Takes a penetrating look at [contemporary sexual chaos]. Passion, celibacy, marriage, fidelity are just some of the subjects that Diana Amsterdam hilariously examines."—Tribune News.   **(#8149)**

ADVICE FROM A CATERPILLAR. (Little Theatre.) Comedy. Douglas Carter Beane. 2m. 2f. 1 Unit set & 1 Int. Ally Sheedy and Dennis Christopher starred in the delightful off-Broadway production of this hip new comedy. Ms. Sheedy played Missy, an avant garde video artist who specializes in re-runs of her family's home videos, adding her own disparaging remarks. Needless to say, she is very alienated from the middle-class, family values she grew up with, which makes her very *au courant*, but strangely unhappy. She has a successful career and a satisfactory love-life with a businessman named Suit. Suit's married, but that doesn't stop him and Missy from carrying on. Something's missing, though—and Missy isn't sure what it is, until she meets Brat. He is a handsome young aspiring actor. Unfortunately, Brat is also the boyfriend of Missy's best friend. Sound familiar? It isn't—because Missy's best friend is a gay man named Spaz! Spaz has been urging Missy to find an unmarried boyfriend, but this is too much—too much for Spaz, too much for Suit and, possibly, too much for Missy. Does she *want* a serious relationship (ugh—how bourgeois!)? Can a bisexual unemployed actor actually be her Mr. Wonderful? "Very funny … a delightful evening."—Town & Village.   **(#3876)**

THE FILM SOCIETY
Jon Robin Baitz
(Little Theatre) Dramatic comedy
4m., 2f. Various ints. (may be unit set)

Imagine the best of Simon Gray crossed with the best of Athol Fugard. The New York critics lavished praise upon this wonderful play, calling Mr. Baitz a major new voice in our theatre. *The Film Society*, set in South Africa, is *not* about the effects of apartheid—at least, overtly. Blenheim is a provincial private school modeled on the second-rate British education machine. It is 1970, a time of complacency for everyone but Terry. a former teacher at Blenheim, who has lost his job because of his connections with Blacks (he invited a Black priest to speak at commencement). Terry tries to involve Jonathan, another teacher at the school and the central character in this play; but Jonathan cares only about his film society, which he wants to keep going at all costs—even if it means programming only safe, non-objectionable, films. When Jonathan's mother, a local rich lady, promises to donate a substantial amount of money to Blenheim if Jonathan is made Headmaster, he must finally choose which side he is on: Terry's or The Establishment's. "Using the school as a microcosm for South Africa, Baitz explores the psychological workings of repression in a society that has to kill its conscience in order to persist in a course of action it knows enough to abhor but cannot afford to relinquish."—New Yorker. "What distinguishes Mr. Baitz' writing, aside from its manifest literacy, is its ability to embrace the ambiguities of political and moral dilemmas that might easily be reduced to blacks and whites."—N.Y. Times. "A beautiful, accomplished play . . . things I thought I was a churl still to value or expect—things like character, plot and theatre dialogue—really do matter."—N.Y. Daily News.   (#8123)

THE SUBSTANCE OF FIRE
Jon Robin Baitz
(Little Theatre.) Drama
3m., 2f. 2 Ints.

Isaac Geldhart, the scion of a family-owned publisher in New York which specializes in scholarly books, suddenly finds himself under siege. His firm is under imminent threat of a corporate takeover, engineered by his own son, Aaron, who watches the bottom line and sees the firm's profitability steadily declining. Aaron wants to publish a trashy novel which will certainly bring in the bucks; whereas Isaac wants to go on publishing worthy scholarly efforts such as his latest project, a multi-volume history of Nazi medical experiments during the Holocaust. Aaron has the bucks to effectively wrench control of the company from his father—or, rather, he has the yen (Japanese businessmen are backing him). What he needs are the votes of the other minority shareholders: his brother Martin and sister Sarah. Like Aaron, they have lived their lives under the thumb of Isaac's imperiousness; and, reluctantly, they agree to side with Aaron against the old man. In the second act, we are back in the library of Isaac's townhouse, a few years later. Isaac has been forcibly retired and has gotten so irascible and eccentric that he may possibly be *non compos mentis*. His children think so, which is why they have asked a psychiatric social worker from the court to interview Isaac to judge his competence. Isaac, who has survived the Holocaust and the death of his wife to build an important publishing company from scratch, must now face his greatest challenge—to persuade Marge Hackett that he is sane. "A deeply compassionate play."—N.Y. Times. "A remarkably intelligent drama. Baitz assimilates and refracts this intellectual history without stinting either on heart or his own original vision."—N.Y. Newsday.   (#21379)

MIXED FEELINGS
(Little Theatre—Comedy)

Donald Churchill
m., 2 f., Int.

This is a riotous comedy about divorce, that ubiquitous, peculiar institution which so shapes practically everyone's life. Arthur and Norma, ex-spouses, live in separate apartments in the same building. Norma has second thoughts about her on-going affair with Arthur's best-friend; while Arthur isn't so sure he wants to continue *his* dalliance with Sonia, wife of a manufacturer with amusingly kinky sexual tastes (Dennis—the manufacturer—doesn't mind that his wife is having an affair; just so long as she continues to provide him with titillating accounts of it while he is dressed as a lady traffic cop). Most of Sonia's accounts are pure fiction, which seems to keep Dennis happy. Comic sparks are ignited into full-fledged farcical flames in the second act, when Dennis arrives in Arthur's flat for lessons in love from the legendary Arthur! "Riotous! A domestic laught romp! A super play. You'll laugh all the way home, I promise you.'—Eastbourne News. "Very funny ... a Churchill comedy that most people will thoroughly enjoy."—The Stage. Restricted New York City.

THE DECORATOR
(Little Theatre/Comedy)

Donald Churchill
m., 2 f., Int.

Much to her surprise, Marcia returns home to find that her flat has not been painted, as she arranged. In fact, the job hasn't even been started yet. There on the premises is the housepainter who is filling in for his ill colleague. As he begins work, there is a surprise visitor--the wife of the man with whom Marcia is having an affair, who has come to confront her nemesis and to exact her revenge by informing Marcia's husband of his wife's infidelity. Marcia is at her wit's end about what to do, until she gets a brilliant idea. It seems the housepainter is a part-time professional actor. Marcia hires him to impersonate her husband, Reggie, at the big confrontation later that day, when the wronged wife plans to return and spill the beans. Hilarity is piled upon hilarity as the housepainter, who takes his acting *very* seriously, portrays the absent Reggie. The wronged wife decides that the best way to get back at Marcia would be to sleep with her "husband" (the house painter), which is an ecstatic experience for them both. When Marcia learns that the housepainter/actor/husband has slept with her rival, she demands to have the opportunity to show the housepainter what *really* good sex is. "This has been the most amazing day of my life", says the sturdy painter, as Marcia leads him into her bedroom. "Irresistible."—London Daily Telegraph.

Other Publications for Your Interest

OTHER PEOPLE'S MONEY
(LITTLE THEATRE—DRAMA)

By JERRY STERNER

3 men, 2 women—One Set

Wall Street takeover artist Lawrence Garfinkle's intrepid computer is going "tilt" over the undervalued stock of New England Wire & Cable. He goes after the vulnerable company, buying up its stock to try and take over the company at the annual meeting. If the stockholders back Garfinkle, they will make a bundle—but what of the 1200 employees? What of the local community? Too bad, says Garfinkle, who would then liquidate the company—take the money and run. Set against the charmingly rapacious financier are Jorgenson, who has run the company since the Year One and his chief operations officer, Coles, who understands, unlike the genial Jorgenson, what a threat Garfinkle poses to the firm. They bring in Kate, a bright young woman lawyer, who specializes in fending off takeovers—and who is the daughter of Jorgenson's administrative assistant, Bea. Kate must not only contend with Garfinkle—she must also move Jorgenson into taking decisive action. Should they use "greenmail"? Try to find a "White Knight"? Employ a "shark repellent"? This compelling drama about Main Street vs. Wall Street is as topical and fresh as today's headlines, giving its audience an inside look at what's *really going on* in this country and asking trenchant questions, not the least of which is whether a corporate raider is really the creature from the Black Lagoon of capitalism or the Ultimate Realist come to save business from itself.

(#17064)

THE DOWNSIDE
(LITTLE THEATRE—COMEDY)

By RICHARD DRESSER

6 men, 2 women—Combination Interior

These days, American business is a prime target for satire, and no recent play has cut as deep, with more hilarious results, than this superb new comedy from the Long Wharf Theatre, Mark & Maxwell, a New Jersey pharmaceuticals firm, has acquired U.S. rights to market an anti-stress drug manufactured in Europe, pending F.D.A. approval; but the marketing executives have got to come up with a snazzy ad campaign by January—and here we are in December! The irony is that nowhere is this drug more needed than right there at Mark & Maxwell, a textbook example of corporate ineptitude, where it seems all you have to do to get ahead is look good in a suit. The marketing strategy meetings get more and more pointless and frenetic as the deadline approaches. These meetings are "chaired" by Dave, the boss, who is never actually there—he is a voice coming out of a box, as Dave phones in while jetting to one meeting or another, eventually directing the ad campaign on his mobile phone while his plane is being hijacked! Doesn't matter to Dave, though—what matters is the possible "downside" of this new drug: hallucinations. "Ridiculous", says the senior marketing executive Alan: who then proceeds to tell how Richard Nixon comes to his house in the middle of the night to visit . . . "Richard Dresser's deft satirical sword pinks the corporate image repeatedly, leaving the audience amused but thoughtful."—Meriden Record. "Funny and ruthlessly cynical."—Phila. Inquirer. "A new comedy that is sheer delight."—Westport News. "The Long Wharf audience laughed a lot, particularly those with office training. But they were also given something to ponder about the way we get things done in America these days, or rather pretend to get things done. No wonder the Japanese are winning."—L.A. Times.

(#6718)

Other Publications for Your Interest

SPOILS OF WAR
(LITTLE THEATRE—DRAMA)

By MICHAEL WELLER

3 men, 3 women—Various Interior settings

Heretofore best known as the author of trenchant, bittersweet comedies such as *Loose Ends* and *Moonchildren*, as well as the screenplays for *Hair* and *Ragtime*, Mr. Weller is here in a deeper, more somber mode, as he chronicles the desperate attempts of a sixteen year-old boy to reconcile his divorced parents. Nobody writes better about disillusionment, about people whose hopes and dreams never quite lived up to reality. In *Moonchildren* and *Loose Ends* Mr. Weller dealt with how the Dream ended up in the sixties and seventies, respectively; here, the fuzzy decade of the fifties is explored through the eyes of Martin's parents, ex-thirties radicals who have chosen very different ways to cope with the changed, changing times. Elyse, the mother, is still a bohemian, a rebel without a cause who wants to live for something more than the rent and the price of hamburger, whereas Andrew, the father, has dropped back into the system, and accepted Life As It Is. And Martin is caught between these finally irreconcilable outlooks, unable to bring his parents back together and wondering what path *his* life will take. "Mr. Weller finds in one family's distintegration a paradigm of the postwar collapse of liberal idealism. This is without question Mr. Weller's most intelligent play, always intelligent and at times moving."—N.Y. Times. "Emotionally charged...a touching, lovely work."—N.Y. Post.

(#21294)

SPEED-THE-PLOW
(ADVANCED GROUPS—SERIOUS COMEDY)

By DAVID MAMET

2 men, 1 woman—Two interior. (may be simply suggested).

This is, without a doubt one of Mamet's best plays (including *American Buffalo* and the stunning, Pulitzer Prize-winning *Glengarry Glen Ross*). Joe Mantegna, Ron Silver and Madonna starred on Broadway in this hilarious and devastating satire of Hollywood, a microcosm of the macrocosm of American culture. Charlie Fox has discovered a terrific vehicle for a certain "hot" male movie star, and has brought it to his "best friend" Bobby Gould, "Head of Production" for a major film company. He coulda taken it across the street; but no, he's brought it to Bobby. Both see the script as their ticket to the really big table, where the real power is. The star wants to do it, and all they have to do is "pitch" it to their boss. The screenplay is a mass of typical action-picture cliches, which they have decided to pitch as a "buddy film"—the current "hot commodity". They'll be taking a meeting with the studio boss tomorrow; but tonight, Bobby has bet Charlie $500 that he can seduce Karen, a temp secretary. His ruse: he has given her a novel "by some Eastern sissy writer" which he has been asked to "courtesy-read" before saying thanks-but-no-thanks. Karen reads the novel and comes to Bobby's house that night—to convince him ... *not* the buddy film, should be the company's next project. Her arguments are ... more so when she agrees to sleep with Bobby, an experience which is ... smogrifying that, much to Charlie's surprise, the next morning he finds ... with Bobby not to put the buddy film "in turnaround", not to pitch the ... m". "By turns hilarious and chilling...[the] dialogue skyrockets."—N.Y. ... clearest, wittiest play."—N.Y. Daily News. "I laughed and laughed. The ... ed with wonderful, dazzling, brilliant lines."—N.Y. Post. "There isn't a line ... ahow insanely funny or scarily insane."—Newsweek.

(#21281)